Building Storage with Style

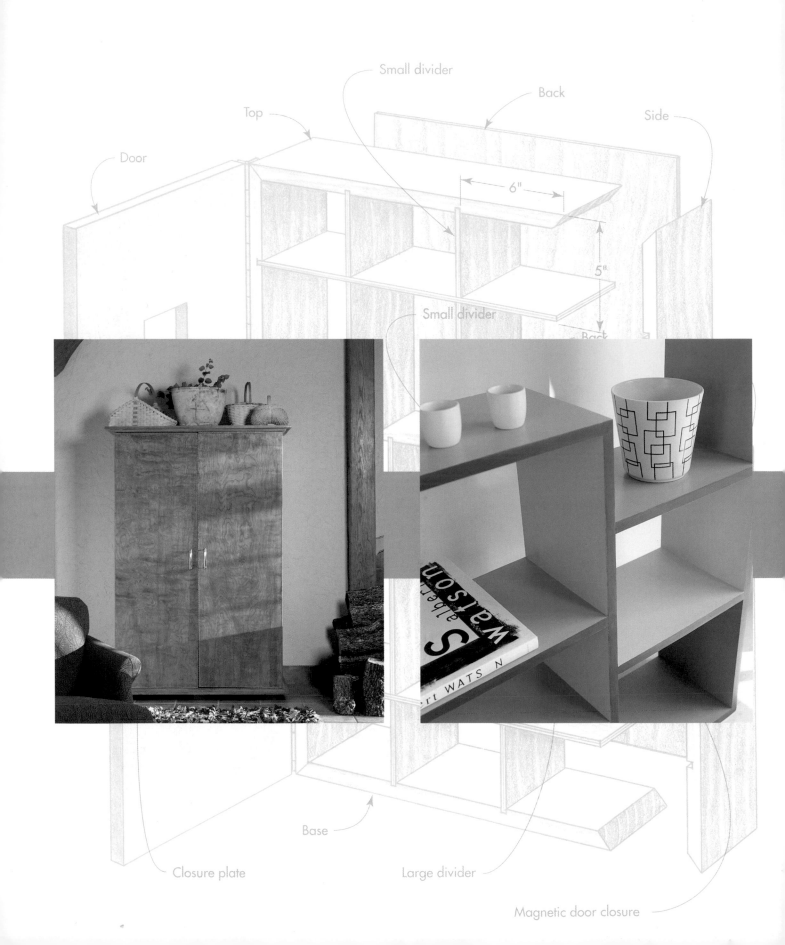

Small divider

Top

Back

Side

Door

6"

5"

Small divider

Back

Base

Closure plate

Large divider

Magnetic door closure

Building Storage with Style

20 Great-Looking Projects from Off-the-Shelf Lumber

Clarke Snell + Lisa Mandle

LARK BOOKS

A Division of Sterling Publishing Co., Inc.
New York

Editor: Suzanne J. E. Tourtillott

Technical Editor: Matthew Teague

Art Director: Dana Irwin

Cover Designer: Barbara Zaretsky

Associate Editor: Nathalie Mornu

Associate Art Director: Shannon Yokeley

Assistant Art Director: Lance Wille

Art Production Assistant: Jeff Hamilton

Editorial Assistance: Delores Gosnell

Art Interns: Ardyce E. Alspach,
Emily Kepley, Nathan Schulman

Illustrator: Frank Rohrbach

Photographer: Stewart O'Shields

We dedicate this book to Rob Pulleyn, esteemed figurehead of Wiseacres, owner of Rob's Pottery Shack, and Crazy Robbie's Wine Store.

Lark thanks the following Asheville, North Carolina, homeowners for letting us use their space to photograph the book's projects: Betty Clark, Kevin and Jo Hogan, Steven Belli, Rob Pulleyn, and Mary Ann West.

These artists' work appears with their permission and our grateful appreciation: on page 36, the trio of paintings is by Margaret Witherspoon, the ceramic work inside the larger Nested Table is by Rob Pulleyn, and George Handy created the ceramic piece atop the smaller Nested Table; on page 72, the painting is by Betty Clark and the bust in the Storage Bench's second cubby from the right is by Sally Kennedy.

Library of Congress Cataloging-in-Publication Data

Snell, Clarke.
  Building storage with style : 20 great-looking projects from off-the-shelf lumber / Clarke Snell & Lisa Mandle.-- 1st ed.
    p. cm.
  Includes index.
  ISBN 1-57990-737-7 (pbk.)
  1. Woodwork--Amateurs' manuals. 2. Storage in the home. I. Mandle, Lisa.
II. Title.
TT185.S5935 2006
684.1'6--dc22

                                                    2005032619

10 9 8 7 6 5 4 3 2 1

First Edition

Published by Lark Books, A Division of
Sterling Publishing Co., Inc.
387 Park Avenue South, New York, N.Y. 10016

Text © 2006, Clarke Snell
Basics and how-to photography © 2006, Clarke Snell unless otherwise specified
Project photography © 2006, Lark Books
Illustrations © 2005, Lark Books

Distributed in Canada by Sterling Publishing,
c/o Canadian Manda Group, 165 Dufferin Street
Toronto, Ontario, Canada M6K 3H6

Distributed in the United Kingdom by GMC Distribution Services,
Castle Place, 166 High Street, Lewes, East Sussex, England BN7 1XU

Distributed in Australia by Capricorn Link (Australia) Pty Ltd.,
P.O. Box 704, Windsor, NSW 2756 Australia

If you have questions or comments about this book, please contact:
Lark Books
67 Broadway, Asheville, NC 28801
(828) 253-0467

Manufactured in China

ISBN 13: 978-1-57990-737-2
ISBN 10: 1-57990-737-7

For information about custom editions, special sales, premium and corporate purchases, please contact Sterling Special Sales Department at 800-805-5489 or specialsales@sterlingpub.com.

Contents

Introduction

It is often said that the modern household should have at least 10 percent of its floor space in storage. Twenty percent is better, and even more is sometimes necessary. Unfortunately, modern housing design doesn't seem to be keeping up with the times. In fact, built-in storage seems to be disappearing from contemporary homes. We've been in many wonderful houses built in the first half of the 20th century that are crawling with storage: multiple closets, recessed book cases, little niches for telephones, bay windows with storage cabinets under the seats, and more. The modern house, on the other hand, often just doesn't grasp the subtle needs of storage. Big walk-in closets and spacious laundry rooms are great, but what's really needed is storage in every room that is designed for very specific purposes.

In this book, our goal is to bridge this storage gap. Clarke and I came up with 20 projects to spread the gospel of good storage throughout your entire house. We've tried to keep the designs simple yet elegant, with clean lines and careful attention to proportion. The result, we hope, is a body of useful furniture and storage solutions that the motivated beginning woodworker can build.

■ IS THIS BOOK FOR YOU?

Okay, so our hope is that this book is appropriate for beginners, but what is a beginning woodworker? Obviously, a baby is a woodworking beginner, but the legal department has asked us to categorically state that babies should not build these projects. What, then, are the prerequisites for starting where this book begins? There is some minimum level of strength you will need to hoist the lumber and partially assembled projects. A basic aptitude with tools, or at least no overt fear of using them, is necessary. We are fans of power tools, so if you are a purist hand tool devotee, these projects may not be for you. If you're completely math-phobic, then this kind of woodworking will drive you crazy because it's all about measuring, adding, and subtracting numbers with $\frac{1}{16}$s, $\frac{1}{8}$s, and the like attached to them. Actually, though, the main things that you'll need are patience and honest desire. If you have these characteristics, the rest of the prerequisites can probably be ignored.

the honest simplicity of these techniques can result in stylish and varied furniture

All of that isn't to say that this book is only for beginners. We think the project designs are interesting and creative enough to be useful to a wide range of readers. If you're an experienced woodworker, let's be upfront from the beginning: our goal here is not elegance of technique, but a sturdy, beautiful end product. We bought all the materials for our projects at our local big-chain building supply store.

For the most part we use simple joints that are fastened most often with glue and screws in visible places. We use wood putty and the occasional wood plugs to fill these holes and other imperfections. If you flip through this book, we think you'll agree that the honest simplicity of these techniques can result in stylish and varied furniture.

Using This Book

If you're a beginner, we'll introduce you to the basic materials, tools, and techniques you'll need to execute these projects in the first chapter, aptly called Basics. This chapter is designed to be read and then referred to often as you approach the individual projects. In addition, take a few minutes to get to know a little about each project in this book before you start building. Look at the how-to photos and illustrations to get a feel for what techniques are being used. We've designed the projects to build slowly on one another, getting incrementally more complex as the book goes on. If you know all the techniques introduced for the previous projects, the next project will only ask that you learn one or two new things. Each project has step-by-step instructions. This isn't great literature, clearly, but we have tried to be clear, concise, and down-to-earth in our descriptions. We've also included detailed drawings that show every part of each project and how it connects with its siblings. Our how-to photography isn't step-by-step, but it is designed to highlight particular details and procedures described in the drawings and written instructions. There is a list of tools, fasteners, and parts for each project, so that you can have everything you need ready to go before you start building.

Though we worked closely together on all aspects of these projects, Clarke drew the short straw, so he's the designated writer. He'll be the voice throughout the rest of this book. He wants to make it clear, though, especially to everyone who knows us and has watched this book take shape, that he's not taking credit! The text just seemed to flow better in the first person, so that's the way he wrote it.

Now, let's make some sawdust!

Basics

To understate, woodworking is a huge topic. Humans have been working with wood for thousands of years, and in that time we've managed to develop a kaleidoscope of materials, techniques, and tools that all fall under the simple title "woodworking." This chapter isn't about all of that. In this chapter, discussion is confined to the basics you'll need to know to build the straightforward projects found in this book. To do that we need to talk about three things: materials, tools, and techniques.

■ MATERIALS

Though woodworking is an intricate art that can be taken to mind-boggling levels of complexity, the projects in this book involve little more than gluing and screwing together store-bought materials. Your projects, then, will only be as good as the resources you choose. Let's take a survey of the materials you'll be using to build the projects in this book.

WOOD. **The main ingredient of the projects in this book is wood. Most of the wood we'll use has been milled into boards, also known as lumber, though some has been more elaborately processed into rigid sheets, appropriately called "sheet materials."**

Lumber

Wood is plant tissue from trees, and lumber is basically any solid piece of wood that has been processed in some way for use in building. Most of these projects are simply pieces of lumber cut and assembled. The myriad species of trees that are harvested to make lumber are divided into two groups: softwood and hardwood. Softwood trees are conifers, what are often called *evergreens*. Most of the lumber you'll find at your local lumberyard is softwoods. Hardwood trees are dicotyledonous…look it up on your own; let's just call them *broad-leaved*. Familiar hardwoods used in building are oak, maple, and cherry. In general, hardwoods are denser and therefore harder than softwoods, but, as is often the case in life, that's not always true. For example, poplar is a very soft hardwood with less density than many softwoods.

Softwoods vs. Hardwoods

Softwood is perfectly suitable for all the projects in this book for several reasons. First, softwoods like pines and spruces are fast growers. This means that they can be grown and harvested more quickly, which in our mass production–fueled economy makes them both cheaper and more common on store shelves. The argument can also be made that using faster-growing trees is easier on the environment because they are more quickly replenished. Second, softer woods are usually easier to work with. Cutting, drilling, screwing, and nailing—the main skills required to build these projects—are all tasks that are easier to perform on softwoods. Third, softer woods are lighter. For some people, the biggest challenge of building these projects will be moving the lumber around. The difference in weight between a shelving unit made of oak and one made of white pine is considerable.

If softwoods are so great, why would anyone use hardwoods? For one thing, hardwoods are often chosen for their beautiful color and wood grain. A carefully finished cherry tabletop can be mesmerizing. In addition, hardwoods are generally more durable, which can be very important for certain types of furniture and other installations. That's why hardwoods such as oak, maple, and walnut are chosen almost exclusively over softwoods to create floor surfaces. Some hardwoods, such as teak, can even withstand the challenges of daily exposure to sun and rain and therefore can be used to make outdoor furniture. However, all of the projects in this book are designed for indoor use and won't be subjected to the abuse that stairs or a kitchen table might be. The strength and durability of most softwoods will be completely adequate for their uses.

Though the woods available in your area may differ slightly from those near me, building supply stores around here carry white pine, southern yellow pine, and some spruce in the dimensions needed to build the projects in this book. Given the choice between those species, I usually prefer yellow pine because it is harder and has a bold, linear grain. White pine, on the other hand, is easy to ding up but very easy to screw and sand. Also, it takes paint well. I tried to mix up the woods a bit in the projects in this book, so that you'd get some idea of what a few species looked like both before and after being finished. A lot of the fun of woodworking is getting to know different woods, so don't be afraid to experiment.

Lumber Dimensions and What They Mean

Dimensioned lumber comes in standard sizes and is always labeled in the same way: thickness first, then width, then length. Usually, the wood species is identified after the dimensions. Therefore, the stack of wood at your local lumber yard labeled "2x10x12, s.y.p." contains southern yellow pine boards that are nominally 2 inches thick, 10 inches wide, and

NOMINAL VS. ACTUAL LUMBER DIMENSIONS

When purchasing lumber, what you see on the label isn't what you get. The actual thickness and width of a piece of lumber is less than what the label says. This is confusing, but at least the relationship between the actual and nominal dimensions is standardized. Looking at the chart and remembering that lumber is always labeled thickness x width x length, you can determine that a 1x4 is actually ¾ inches thick and 3½ inches wide and that a 2x8 is actually 1½ inches thick and 7¼ inches wide. After working with lumber for a while, the numbers in this chart will become second nature.

Thickness		Width	
Nominal (inches)	Actual (inches)	Nominal (inches)	Actual (inches)
1	¾	2	1½
¾	1	4	3½
2	1½	6	5½
		8	7¼
		10	9¼
		12	11¼

12 feet long. I use the word *nominally* because in reality those boards are 1½ inches thick, 9¼ inches wide, and 12 feet plus a ½ inch or so long. That's right, the actual and named (nominal) dimensions of lumber are different! Refer to the Nominal vs. Actual Lumber Dimensions chart, above, to unlock the mysteries of this arcane labeling system.

Lumber can be sold in three ways: by the stick, by the board foot, and by the linear foot. You'll need to know how these systems work in order to compare apples with apples, and be sure that you're getting

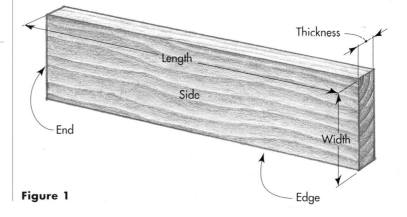

Figure 1

enough material to build a given project. Most lumber you'll buy will be sold by the stick: each piece will be labeled individually with its nominal thickness, width, and length, and you'll pay a single price for the entire board. You'll also find boards sold by the linear foot; a linear foot (l.f.) of lumber is simply a piece of wood of a given thickness and width that is one foot long. For example, a 2x4x10 is 10 linear feet of 2x4. Hardwoods, fancy trims, and lumber at saw mills are often sold by the linear foot. A board foot, on the other hand, isn't a measure of length, but of volume. One board foot of lumber is a piece of wood 1 inch thick, 1 foot wide, and 1 foot long or any combination of dimensions that would constitute the same volume of wood. For example, a ½ inch x 1 foot x 2 foot piece of lumber is also one board foot. Confusing? Chances are you won't come across lumber sold by the board foot in the process of making any of the projects in this book. Just keep it in the back of your mind that there is a huge difference between something labeled "b.f." and something labeled "l.f." If you see "b.f.," tell the salesperson what you need in linear feet and let them do the conversion.

Selecting Lumber

Lumber is produced from a living organism and in many ways it's still alive. It can take on and give off water, which can cause it to swell, shrink, deform, and crack. The lumber you'll find at the local lumberyard has been kiln dried, a process by which most of the water is pulled out of the wood. Kiln drying makes wood more stable, less likely to crack and split, and less interesting to insects. Remember that most of the wood you'll come across is probably designed for building construction, not furniture. That means you'll need to inspect the lumber yourself, choosing boards that are appropriate for the project you intend to build.

Unless you have some specific aesthetic in mind, the best lumber for furniture building is going to be straight and smooth, without checks (cracks through the board that can be caused by the milling or drying process) and with as few knots as possible. Knots are really cross sections of branches. In a piece of lumber, they're essentially separate pieces of wood embedded in the board. They can be hard to screw through, take paint and other finishes differently than the rest of the board, and can simply pop out, leaving a hole.

For a few of these projects I chose cabinet grade lumber, which is selected for its clean grain and absence of knots and other imperfections. Usually, the lumber at a building supply will be separated loosely into grades. All of the rough framing lumber and decking materials will be in one place and the trim and finer grades of lumber will be elsewhere. It's a good idea to spend some time roaming around your local building supply store getting to know the different lumbers and other materials available. Though it is quickest to choose from the cabinet grade lumber, it's also a little more expensive. Often times I'll sift through framing lumber to find the nicest boards.

If a board looks free of inperfections, check next to make sure that it is straight. There are several ways a board can be deformed (see figure 2). Visual inspection for these problems is a skill that you have to develop. Start by sighting down one edge of the board from end to end. This will tell you if the board is crooked. If you have trouble visually inspecting for bowing, cupping, and twisting, set the board face down on the floor and see how flat it lays.

Once you've got your stack of straight, clear boards, do yourself a favor and check the width of each board. In my experience, it isn't uncommon for the actual width of a given board to be as much as $\frac{1}{16}$ inch larger or smaller than the labeled dimension. Make sure all the boards are of uniform width. In other words, it doesn't matter if your 1x10s are in fact $9\frac{3}{16}$ inches wide, as long as they are all $9\frac{3}{16}$ inches wide.

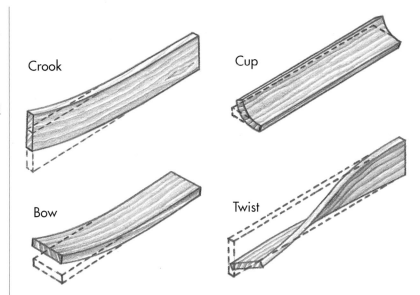

Figure 2

Sheet Materials

The widest lumber commonly available at your local hardware store is $11\frac{1}{4}$ inches wide. What do you do if you need to build something wider? You can either connect two or more pieces of lumber together or you can use one of the myriad wood-based sheet goods presently available.

The most widely known sheet goods are commonly called *plywood*, which are made from thin sheets of wood that are cemented together using strong glues. Unlike lumber that is produced by sawing thick slices through the length of a tree, these thin sheets of wood, called *veneers*, are peeled or sliced off the log. Most plywood is manufactured in sheets 4 feet wide and 8 feet long, and it comes in a variety of thicknesses. The large lumber store chains usually sell partial sheets, so you can often buy a piece close to the size you need. Plywood comes in a variety of grades with higher, more expensive grades having surfaces with fewer imperfections. These higher grades are sometimes called *finish plywood*.

There are a wide variety of other wood-based sheet materials. Some of these, such as OSB (oriented strand board) and MDF (medium density fiberboard), use wood chips or sawdust in combination with glues. Some sheet goods have a core made of these composite materials and an exterior veneer made of wood or some other material. In cases where a project calls for sheet goods, I'll give specific information on the type I recommend.

Fasteners

Now you know that you're going to use a few boards and the occasional piece of plywood. It's time to figure out how to hold that stuff together in the shape of furniture. Enter the fascinating world of fasteners. Like most things in the modern world, there is a mind-boggling array of fasteners to choose from, but I've limited fastening options to a few kinds of screws, a single glue, and the very occasional nail. Still, you'll have to navigate the huge fastener aisle at the hardware store, so I'll give you a bit of basic information on what to look for.

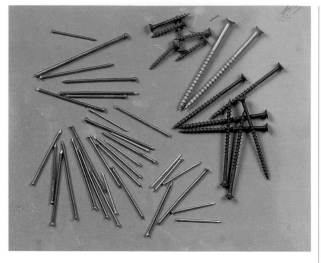

FASTENERS. **Your local hardware store houses a huge menagerie of nails, bolts, screws, and other doodads designed to connect pieces of wood together. Collectively, this cornucopia is called fasteners.**

Nails

Nails consist of a shank and a head. You won't use many nails in these projects because, simply put, they are inferior to screws for your purposes. Nails require a jarring force, i.e., hammering, to install. This pounding can push your carefully cut and aligned joint out of whack. What's worse, if you've messed up your joint by pounding them in, they're very difficult to remove.

Still, nails have their occasional place in these projects. Though there are many kinds of nails, you'll only be using finish nails. Finish nails have a smooth shank and a small head, which is less obtrusive and less likely to split the wood upon entry. The size of finish nails is designated by gauges. The larger the gauge number, the thinner the nail. The length of the nail is usually indicated along with the gauge.

THREE KINDS OF SCREWS. **The screw on the right is a Phillips head, which is easy to strip. The screw in the middle can be driven with either a Phillips head or square-drive bit. The screw on the left has a square-drive head. This particular screw is also known as a *finish screw* because it has a smaller head that is easier to conceal below the finished surface of a project. In all my years of carpentry, I've never stripped a single square-drive screw.**

Screws

For your purposes, screws are an improvement over nails because they have a threaded shaft. Instead of pushing straight in, they twist (or screw!) into the wood, creating a very tight bond. Another advantage of screws is that they have less tendency to push a joint out of alignment than hammered nails. In addition, if something isn't right about a screwed joint, you can unscrew the fastener and try again—a great boon to the beginner.

Okay, so screws are great. Now, here's a piece of advice that's worth the price of this book: unless you're a masochist (hey, to each their own), don't use flat head or Phillips head screws. When used with the now ubiquitous cordless screwdriver whose torque comes from a battery not a twisting forearm, the result too often is a stripped head and a big headache. (A stripped screw head results when the screwdriver can't hold onto the screw and simply spins around, eventually destroying the grooves that allow the driver to grip the screw.) On the other hand, after years of using square-drive screws, I can't remember ever stripping one. I suggest using square-drive screws for all of these projects, and just about any other project you tackle.

Most of the screws used in this book are pictured at left. Finish and deck screws (the lion's share of what you'll use) are easy to choose because they usually have the same shaft diameter—simply look for the length you need. Many screws, however, come in both different lengths and shaft diameters, called *gauges*. The smaller the gauge, the smaller the shaft. A screw of gauge 0 has a shaft $\frac{1}{16}$ inch in diameter while a 5-gauge screw has a $\frac{1}{8}$ inch shaft. The only time you'll need to be conscious of the gauge is when a specific gauge is designated.

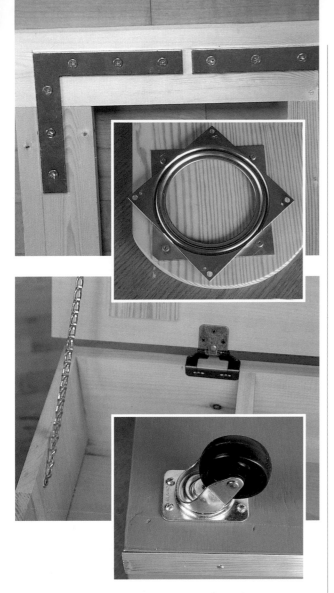

Hardware

What is hardware? In the context of this book, it's a grab-bag term referring to anything that is bought as a unit and attached to a project. Most of the hardware is installed to allow movement. For example, casters allow a project to roll, hinges allow doors to swing, and handles allow doors to be pulled out. You can also install hardware that lets you to hang projects on a wall.

I have made every effort to choose hardware that is easy to install. However, you may be unable to find exactly what is used in this book. In addition,

choosing different hardware is an easy way to adjust the look of these projects to fit your own taste, something that I wholeheartedly encourage.

Here are a few basic tips for your forays into the hardware aisle. First, buy quality. Even the most basic woodworking project will take a fair amount of your precious time. There is nothing more frustrating than carefully building something, only to have a hinge bend or a handle break one day out of the blue. I'm a frugal person, but I've never regretted for a second buying the best hardware for anything I've built. Second, buy more than you need. If you're not sure which handle will look better, buy both of them. If you forgot to check exactly how wide that hinge needs to be, buy a variety. As long as you don't damage the merchandise, you can return whatever you don't use. Nothing will slow the momentum of a project like multiple trips to the hardware store. Third, ask for help. Today's mega-hardware store is basically a massive warehouse that the customer is allowed to rummage around in. Finding a specific little hinge in that huge haystack can be a demoralizing quest.

■ TOOLS

You now know that these projects are going to be made out of a few boards fastened together and the occasional piece of hardware attached. Next, you need to think about the tools you'll use to cut and attach these pieces together.

Of course, tools are a huge topic chock full of history, potential debate, and lots and lots of possibilities. Let's stay focused. What tools do you really need to complete the projects in this book? In a group of woodworkers, even this simple question would set off endless debate. I'll give you my perspective here, but there is more than one way to cut any given board—it's up to you to decide whether my suggestions are right for your situation.

WORKING GREEN?

I'm concerned about the impact I have on the environment, so I try to carefully choose materials for any projects I build. In my opinion, when processed and used sensibly, wood is an environmentally sound choice. Since wood is the main ingredient of the projects in this book, then we're already ahead of the game. Still, all wood and wood products available for sale are not created equal. If you're concerned about conserving resources and reducing your effect on the environment, here are some basic tips for choosing wood:

1. Buy local. The less distance lumber has to travel to get from where it's grown to your doorstep, the less effect it will have. If you live in a forested area, chances are that there are nearby sawmills cutting locally harvested lumber. If there is a kiln on site for drying the milled boards, then you should be able to buy lumber similar to what you see in the photos in this book for reasonable prices. Of course, many of us don't live near forests. In that case, you can still ask your local lumberyard where the wood they sell comes from. If enough people ask, they may become more conscious of the issue themselves.

2. Look for sustainably harvested lumber. Put simply, lumber is sustainably harvested when trees are cut and processed in a way that is least destructive to the local ecosystem, which in turn allows the forest to continue producing more trees for harvest. A nonprofit organization called the Forest Stewardship Council (FSC) has developed certification guidelines to evaluate lumber production. Many large hardware stores and lumberyards are starting to carry FSC-certified lumber, so simply look for the label when shopping for lumber. By choosing FSC lumber, you'll not only be improving the environmental impact of your coffee table or bookshelf, but you'll be letting the store know that you want environmentally friendly products.

3. Avoid toxins. Strangely enough, many wood-based construction materials include poisons. Formaldehyde glues in sheet materials and volatile organic compounds (VOCs) in paints are just a couple examples. Fortunately, there are almost always alternatives. Learn about what you are about to buy. If it contains toxins, look for a substitute.

4. Waste not, want not. This advice may sound obvious, but a perusal of construction sites and furniture manufacturing shops will quickly prove its novelty. In the real world, LOTS of construction materials go to waste. To break free of this trend, take the extra time to get organized. If you plan on building several projects, combine their parts lists in such a way to get the most out of the lengths of lumber and sizes of sheet materials available on the hardware store shelves. In addition, keep an eye out for salvage. For example, I almost guarantee that you can find the plywood used in most of our projects piled in the trash bin at a construction site near you.

Tool Recommendations

Here are the tools I recommend for completing the projects in this book. You'll need all the tools in the Necessities list (or something comparable) to complete almost any project. For example, if you can cut straight and true with a hand saw, then it's comparable to and could conceivably replace a circular saw. I, on the other hand, don't have the skill to rip an inch off the width of an 8-foot-long 2x6 with a hand saw. I imagine that the same is true for most people reading this book, so I suggest just buying everything in the first list. Strongly Recommended tools will make your projects go a lot faster and allow the beginner to achieve better results.

Necessities

Circular saw with rip fence

Cordless drill

Speed square or combination square

Framing square

Straight edge

Measuring tape

Clamps

Mallet

Sharp pencil

Eye and ear protection

Strongly Recommended

Powered miter saw

Table saw

Random-orbit sander

Jigsaw

Tool belt

13-ounce finish hammer

Really Nice to Have

Japanese crosscut saw

Router

Every hand tool known to humanity

Power vs. Hand Tools

Perhaps contrary to common sense, I think power tools are made for beginners. Why? There are several reasons. First, power tools require substantially less skill to master than hand tools. Something as simple as cutting a wide board very accurately to length is a real skill with a hand saw. It requires a well-tuned saw and a fair amount of experience to make a clean enough cut even for these simple projects. After getting over the initial trepidation that sensibly arises in the presence of a rapidly spinning blade, the same cut can be mastered quickly with a circular saw. With a powered miter saw, the cut requires little more skill than being able to set a board on a flat surface.

Second, I believe that power tools match the mindset of most people reading this book. Aren't you more interested in getting some furniture built than learning a fascinating, Zen-like hand tool skill that will help you improve as a person? If so, power tools are for you. They allow you to get things done faster.

Third, some of the techniques and materials that I specify in these projects simply demand power tools. For example, there is no practical way for a beginner to accurately rip 2 inches off the length of a 2x10x10 with a hand saw. The same goes for cutting a 4x8 sheet of plywood in half. If you have to buy the tools for these tasks, why not make life easier and use them for other tasks?

But power tools have their downsides. First, of course, they are potentially very dangerous. Though the power tools I recommend in this book are easy to use, it is imperative that you learn the correct

techniques for operating them and follow basic safety procedures religiously. Second, power tools are loud and make more mess than hand tools. Finally, they are part of the automation frenzy that is sweeping our culture. Wood is a very subtle, sensuous material and part of the fun of working it is to feel it, to get intimate with it. Power tools make things easier, but they are also blunt and impersonal, creating a separation between you and the wood. If your interest in woodworking grows, I suggest slowly expanding your experience to include more and more hand tools. You can take this quest as far as you like. My brother-in-law is an accomplished furniture maker who uses no power tools or even sandpaper, creating an incredibly fine finished surface for exquisite furniture by using a succession of hand planes.

Whatever tools you choose, make sure you buy quality. If you take care of them, good tools will last a lifetime. With that in mind, also spend a bit of cash on your tool storage. Get a nice size toolbox—once you get into tools, you'll always want more. As for power tools, cordless versions have sprouted like weeds over the last 20 years and it's now possible to go almost completely cordless. The higher the voltage, the heavier the tool—so it's not always necessary to choose the tool with the most power. One of the best power tool innovations in recent memory is the electric brake. This feature actively brakes a tool after you let go of the trigger rather than letting it slowly wind down through the forces of friction and gravity. If a tool is available with a brake, put out the extra cash for that model. Also, if your tool doesn't come with a case, do yourself a favor and shell out a few extra bucks for one.

Measuring + Marking Tools

The first steps in most projects is measuring and marking something to be cut. To do that, you'll need a measuring tape, speed square or combination square, and a sharp pencil. Make sure that you buy a quality measuring tape at least 16 feet long. The tape itself should be thick and the housing strong.

Another important measuring tool is an L-shaped ruler, or framing square. It can also be used as a straightedge to draw lines and as a guide to determine whether or not a joint is square.

Cutting Tools

Making larger boards into smaller boards is the key to woodworking, and there are a number of tools available.

Powered Saws

You'll need either a circular saw or miter saw to make any of the projects in this book. It's definitely better to have both. The motor and blade of a powered miter saw is mounted on a table, and the blade moves up and down on a spring-loaded hinge. You hold the board with one hand and operate the saw with the other. Cuts are quick, easy, and very accurate. Miter saws come in a variety of shapes and sizes. Sliding miter saws have the motor and blade mounted on a rod that you push through the wood. These saws can cut wider boards than fixed miter saws. Compound miter saws can be adjusted to cut angles both vertically and horizontally to the board. I made most of the cuts for these projects using a simple, fixed miter saw, but a sliding or compound miter saw might come in handy for later projects.

Circular saws are handheld and mobile, which makes them popular in the construction of buildings where you often need to take the saw to the cut. But mobility and human error makes them less accurate and more difficult to operate than a miter saw. In building these projects, I used a circular saw for occasional rip cuts and a few other cuts. To rip with a circular saw, you can either use a straightedge to guide the saw or use an attachment aptly named a *rip fence*. A rip fence is a T-shaped piece of metal that guides the saw in a straight line by cradling an existing straight edge of the board being cut. Rip fences attach through a slot in the circular saw where the distance of the guide from the blade can

POWER SAWS. **The saw at the top of the photo is a miter saw (sometimes called a *chop saw*). It consists of a motor spinning a blade mounted in a hinged assembly that allows for a variety of angled cuts. The saw in the middle is a circular saw, which is basically a motor spinning a saw blade enclosed in a handheld case. The saw in the foreground is a jigsaw. The blades in a jigsaw move up and down, allowing for a range of curves and other cuts that are impossible with other power saws.**

be adjusted and fixed by tightening a setscrew. Make sure that the circular saw you buy can accept a rip fence.

Though you can rip with a circular saw, in most situations a table saw is superior for this job. I used a full-size shop model, which is known as a *contractor's saw*, but the small portable table saws (often referred to as *bench-top table saws*) are inexpensive and will handle any of the projects in this book. If you buy one, I suggest attaching it securely to a work table before cutting. It's also very handy to have a powered jigsaw. Jigsaws have a blade that moves up and down. This allows you to cut in tight places, turn corners while cutting , and cut curves easily.

There are a variety of blades available for each of these saws. The main things that distinguish different wood cutting blades are the width of the teeth, called the *kerf*, and the number of teeth. Blades are designed for various materials and types of cuts, but a moderately priced combination blade should be more than sufficient for both rips and crosscuts in wood. If possible, choose a carbide-toothed blade— they last much longer.

Hand Saws

Though I recommend using power saws for most of the cuts in this book, hand saws have a lot to recommend them. They are quiet, light, and fun to use. You feel a lot more connection to the material cutting with a hand saw. If you're going to buy only one hand saw, make it a Japanese design because they cut on the pull stroke rather than the push stroke, which makes them a lot easier to control. Don't take my word for it; do a side-by-side test and I'm pretty sure you'll be convinced. Also consider purchasing a miter box, which consists of a handsaw attached to an assembly that allows for a variety of angled cuts. These tools range from a plastic box with slits cut in it to a precision mechanism very similar to powered miter saws. These saws are generally designed for cutting trim and therefore won't cut very thick or very wide boards.

Drills

Okay, let's cut to the chase: Buy a cordless drill. In my opinion, this tool is perhaps one of the best inventions in the last 50 years. But there are way too many varieties of cordless drills to choose from. For your purposes, however, a 12-volt model has plenty of power. Make sure it has at least two speeds and a keyless chuck, which will allow you to change bits and drivers quickly.

You'll also need an assortment of drill bits for boring holes. They can be bought separately or in cased sets arranged in

DRILLS, BITS, AND DRIVERS. **To build the projects in this book, you'll need a drill and an assortment of bits and drivers.**

HAND SAWS. **The saw at top right is the archetypal hand saw that most of us are familiar with. The teeth on this saw cut as the saw is pushed through the wood. If you think about it, that's a strange design idea: pushing a thin piece of metal through a hard piece of wood. The teeth of Japanese hands saws, like the one pictured above, cut as the blade is being pulled through the wood. This uses the intrinsic strength of the blade very efficiently. The result is less effort and less binding of the blade while cutting.**

order of size. For starters, look for a set with bits ranging from $\frac{1}{16}$ inch up to $\frac{1}{4}$ inch. To drill larger holes, you'll need auger, spade, or Forstner bits. Auger bits have a large spiraling cutting edge. They are aggressive, which means they cut quickly, but they are also expensive. Spade bits have a shaft that widens into a wide flat blade of a given diameter. The blade is sharpened along the edge. Sets of spade bits are inexpensive and offer a variety of diameters. On the down side, spade bits have a protruding point that makes them difficult to use for cutting holes that don't go completely through the wood. They also have a tendency to tear out the bottom of the hole they cut. Forstner bits solve both of these problem, but tend to be more expensive than spade bits. For even larger holes, you'll need hole saws. These are circular bits with teeth all around their circumference. Although these can be pricy, inexpensive hole saw kits containing a variety of blades are available.

In addition to bits, you'll need a variety of drivers for driving screws. Drivers hold the heads of screws and twist them into the wood. It's a good idea to buy a set containing a wide variety of drivers in different sizes.

Clamps

A clamp is an extra pair of hands. A group of clamps is an obedient crew of workers. You'll be using clamps for a variety of purposes—securing materials to work surfaces, securing joints in place before screwing, and various other tasks. Clamping is an intuitively obvious procedure but it takes a bit of practice to master—don't get discouraged if you're clumsy at first. There is a wide array of clamp types and sizes to choose from. To complete the projects in this book, I recommend buying at least a couple of 12-inch quick-grip clamps, at least two 36-inch bar clamps, a corner clamp, and a few small spring clamps. However, clamps are relatively inexpensive, so the more the merrier. Look for

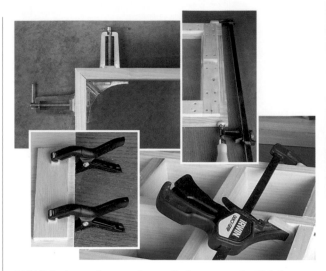

CLAMPS. **I used a variety of clamps to build the projects in this book. Clockwise from top right: bar clamp, quick-grip clamp, spring clamps, corner clamp.**

clamps with padded clamping faces so that they won't mar the surface of the wood.

Sanders

There are different ways to sand. For example, you can go with the age-old, low-tech method of sandpaper wrapped around a wood block. However, I strongly recommend investing in an electric random-orbit sander. This tool moves the sandpaper across the wood in a complex pattern that aggressively removes wood while creating an even finish. These sanders are available with either 5-inch or 6-inch discs. Buy a model that accepts hook-and-loop sanding discs, which allow you to remove a disc and then reuse it later. Also, make sure that your sander has a bag for dust collection. Even with such an attachment, these sanders will put dust into the air, so always wear a dust mask. My sander also has a speed adjustment, which comes in handy for various operations.

■ THE WORKSPACE

If you're going to be doing any woodworking, you should accept one thing up front—it makes a mess.

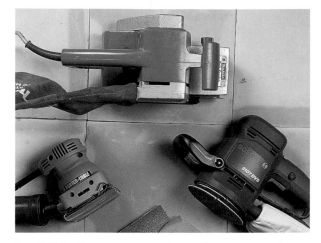

SANDERS. **There are a variety of power sanders available, each appropriate for a specific job. For the projects in this book, I recommend using a random-orbit sander like the one at the right side of this photo.**

If you go into a professional woodworking shop, you'll probably see all sorts of hoses crawling up from the tools and along the walls and ceiling. These are part of an expensive system whose sole purpose is to collect the sawdust created from cutting wood. You probably don't have that luxury, so your work is going to put sawdust into the air that will eventually land on every horizontal surface in the surrounding area. In other words, it's not going to cut it to just push the living room couch out of the way to set up a weekend workshop. It's a moot point anyway because chances are that the room is too small in any case.

That brings up another point: woodworking takes space. Most of the lumber you'll be using will be 8 to 12 feet long. You need to be able to turn boards around freely, set up separate work areas for cutting and assembly, as well as store materials, fasteners, and tools. If you have the room outside you can set up a nice, sunny-day workshop. If you've got a big covered porch, that can work too. Of course, garages and basements, the old standbys, are probably going to be your best bet. Whatever your situation, do yourself a favor and set up a decent workspace before attempting any project.

Safety Equipment

Whether hand or powered, woodworking tools can be very dangerous. Anyone who works professionally with wood, either in construction or furniture, knows people who have injured themselves with tools. First of all, you need comfortable eye and ear protection. You should pick glasses that are light and unobtrusive because once you walk into your woodshop, you should rarely take them off. The same goes for ear protection. You aren't going to use it if you have to look around and find it before turning on a tool. That doesn't mean you have to have them over your ears all the time. Many types of ear protection can sit comfortably around your neck when not in use. It's also important to have some sort of dust mask or respirator for certain activities. The basic, cheap, disposable dust mask is only partially effective. You may want to invest in a quality respirator. Whether you use a dust mask or a respirator depends on the kind of work you do, how often you do it, and the ventilation of your work area.

■ TECHNIQUES

Now that you know the basics about the materials these projects will be made of and the tools you'll use to make them, all you need to figure out is how

SAFETY. **As someone who has had to have pieces of wood and metal removed from an eye on three different building-related occasions, I know the meaning of the phrase "safety first." The drill is simple: (1) buy ear, eye, and lung protection; (2) USE THEM!!**

to use the tools to turn the materials into furniture. In other words, you need to learn some basic woodworking techniques.

Joinery

The method by which materials are cut and connected together is known as *joinery*. In some woodworking, joinery is a complex, artful process that involves shaping pieces of wood to lock together. For these projects, I took the simpler route of connecting most joints with applied fasteners, usually screws or nails in combination with glue. The extent of joinery techniques you need to understand, then, is how to cut and prepare two pieces of wood so that they can sit flush against one another and accept the fasteners of choice.

Measuring and Marking

The first step you'll take in the joining process is measuring and marking the wood to be cut. There are several helpful tricks to making accurate measurements. First, mark the length with a crow's foot, basically an arrow pointing at the number on the tape—a simple slash or dot is too easy to misinterpret. Second, draw a line along the full length of the cut whenever possible. This will allow you to follow the progress of your cut. For simple crosscuts, you can use a speed square to mark cuts

FINDING THE MIDDLE

Here's an easy method for accurately finding the middle of a board. First, measure the full length of the board. Divide this measurement in half. Pull your tape from one end of the board and make a crow's foot at the calculated middle. Now pull your tape from the other end of the board. If you calculated correctly, your crow's foot should be pointing to the same number on the tape. If you're off a bit, adjust the crow's foot accordingly. Pull the tape from both ends of the board again to check your new mark.

quickly and accurately. Finally, double-check your measurement after you've drawn the line. The tired old carpenter's saying "measure twice, cut once" is tired and old because it's true. If you ignore this advice, you'll quickly come back to the fold after you've miscut a number of boards and had to slink back to the lumber store for more material. One particular malady to watch out for is "inch-itus," the mysterious and common affliction for adding or subtracting an inch from a given measurement.

Cutting

The next step toward joining wood is to cut it. The cutting for fancy joinery can get pretty involved, but this book calls for only a few basic techniques. Mostly you'll cut only to change the length or width of a board. Here are the basic cuts you'll use.

CROSSCUTTING

Crosscutting is cutting across the grain of the wood, i.e., through the width of a board and it's by far the most common cut you'll use in this book. Most crosscuts will be made at 90 degrees to the side of the board, and so are called *square* or *butt cuts*. Here's the basic procedure for making a square cut:

- **Inspect the board.** Look for imperfections and knots. If there are any sections of the board that seem too bad to use, make a large, bold X through the area. Remove any staples and labels.

- **Plan your cuts.** When possible make all cuts in order, from longest to shortest. That way, if you mess up a long cut you can cut the board again to become one of the project's shorter pieces. Loosely lay out your cuts on the board before you begin. If you marked any bad spots with Xs, see if you can arrange cuts to get the maximum out of the board while avoiding the bad area. Also, if at all possible, don't cut near a knot. Having a knot near a joint might force you to screw or nail through it, which often causes boards to split.

PRECISION HANDHELD CROSSCUTS. **Crosscutting with a circular saw is easier and more precise if you use your speed square as a handheld guide.**

• **Square the end.** Before measuring, use your speed square to make sure that the end of the board is square and smooth. If it isn't, mark the board near the end and make the purpose of your first crosscut be to square the board. Double-check the end of the board, making sure you've removed any labels or staples.

• **Measure, mark, and cut.** Measure and mark the board as described previously, making sure to pull the tape from the squared end. Using a hand, circular, or powered miter saw, cut the board on the outer edge of the line (i.e., the edge farthest from where the measuring tape started). If you use a circular saw, hold a speed square in place next to the saw's foot (the flat metal piece that sits on the board) as a guide while you cut. Note: If your miter saw can't cut through the entire width of the board, cut as far as you can, then flip the board over to finish the cut.

Occasionally, you'll make a miter cut—a crosscut at 45 degrees—to either the thickness or the face of the board. The easiest way to make a miter cut is with a miter saw. The saw is adjusted to the angle and then the cut is made with the same ease as a square cut.

Most circular saws can also be adjusted to cut at an angle to the surface of the board, so you don't necessarily have to have a miter saw to make a miter cut.

RIPPING

Sometimes you'll need a piece of lumber that has a different width than the available standards. In this case, you'll cut along the grain of the wood, i.e., along the length of the board. This is called a *rip cut*. Cutting sheet materials also requires a rip cut. For beginners and other mere mortals, the only saws practical for making the rips needed in these projects are either a circular saw with a rip fence or a table saw. Ripping with a table saw consists only

HANDHELD RIPS. **A circular saw outfitted with a rip fence is a convenient way to make accurate rip cuts. The outer edge of the fence then holds the saw in a straight line relative to the side of the board as the saw cuts. The fence can be adjusted and set using a screw attached to the foot of the saw.**

of setting the guide, or fence, the correct distance away from the blade and then pushing the wood against the fence and past the blade. Ripping with a circular saw is more involved, so I'll describe the process in a bit more detail:

• **Mark the cut.** Draw a line along the entire cut by marking both ends of the board and connecting the two points by using a straightedge such as a level or straight board. This will allow you to keep track of your cut as you go.

• **Place the board.** Clamp the wood securely to your worktable. Avoid cutting the table surface by lifting the piece up on blocks or making sure that the cut overhangs the edge of the table.

• **Prepare the saw.** Adjust the blade depth so that it will extend only 1/8 inch past the bottom of the board while cutting. Set the rip fence in place so that its guide is to the right if your saw has its motor on the left, and vice versa if it has its motor on the right.

• **Make the cut.** If the motor of your saw is on the left, approach the board so that the piece you will keep is on the left. Reverse this if your saw has a motor on the right. This is done so that you can see the line as you are cutting. Adjust the rip fence so that it will hold the blade tight to the side of the line farthest from the part of the board you intend to keep. Making sure that the blade isn't touching the board, depress the trigger to start the blade spinning. Keep the rip fence guide snug against the side of the board and push the saw through the wood with a slow, steady motion.

CUTTING GROOVES

On a few occasions, it's necessary to cut a groove in a piece of wood. You'll use two basic groove cuts in this book. Many woodworkers dicker over the terms used, but for the sake of simplicity, this book calls any groove cut through the middle of a board so

that it has three sides a *dado*. A groove cut at the end or edge of a board—so that it has two sides—is called a *rabbet*. The easiest and most accurate method for cutting a groove is to use a table saw fitted with a cluster of blades, called a *dado blade*, that together equal the width of your desired groove. If you don't have a dado blade, you can also cut a groove with a circular saw, a router, or a single blade on a table saw. Here's how:

TWO KINDS OF GROOVES. **Three-sided grooves (above) are called *dadoes* and two-sided grooves (below) are referred to as *rabbets*.**

• **Mark the cut.** First, mark the width of the groove with two pencil lines. The distance between the lines should be a hair (roughly 1/32 inch) larger than the thickness of the board that will fit in the groove.

• **Set the detpth.** Set the blade depth on your tool to cut a groove of the desired depth.

• **Make the cut.** If you're using a circular saw, make a straight cut along each pencil line using a rip fence or a straightedge clamped in place to guide your cut. Then make multiple passes to clean out the wood

CUTTING PLYWOOD

There are several options for making the plywood cuts required for the projects in this book. The easiest is to have your plywood cut where you buy it. Most large building supply stores will make custom cuts for you. Often, the first cut or two are free. These stores also usually have precut partial sheets that will minimize your waste. If you're cutting the sheet goods yourself, the easiest approach is to use a table saw. However, it is also very common to cut plywood with a circular saw. The only difference between ripping lumber and plywood is that the cuts on plywood are often so wide that you're unable to use a rip fence to guide the cut. If that's the case, you can either carefully make the cut freehand or you can set up a simple fence to guide your saw. For a really clean cut, use a rip blade with 40 teeth.

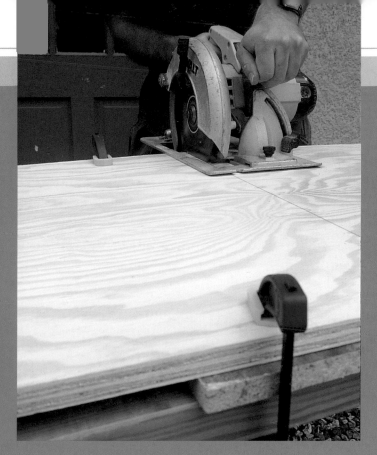

FREEHAND PLYWOOD RIP. Here, plywood is being ripped without the aid of a guide. Notice that the plywood is supported and lifted off the sawhorse. Without this precaution, the plywood will tend to buckle as you cut. This will result in the blade binding in the cut and kicking back toward you, a potentially dangerous proposition.

CUTTING PLYWOOD WITH A GUIDE.
When cutting two pieces to the same length, stack them and use a guide so they will match perfectly. Mark the top piece to length. Measure the distance between your circular saw blade and the outer edge of its foot (the metal plate that sits on the board). Clamp a straight piece of lumber this distance away from the line marking your length. This board should be wide enough to allow a clamp to hold it in place while still leaving room for the saw to pass without hitting the clamp. Make the cut with the circular saw, keeping its foot tight against the guide throughout the cut.

For more precise rips clamp a straightedge to the plywood to act as a guide for the saw as it cuts.

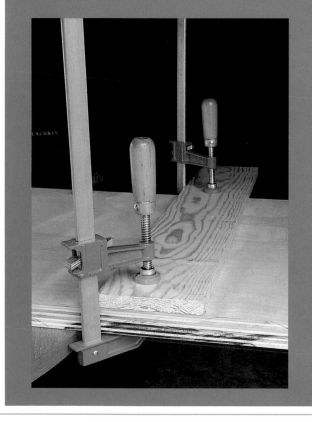

between these two cuts. You don't need to cut in a straight line on these passes, just be careful not to let the saw stray outside the area of the groove. To clean out the last bits of wood, use a chisel.

If using a table saw without a dado blade, set the fence to make the first cut on one side of the groove. Make the cut. Move the fence ⅛ inch in the appropriate direction and make a second cut. Continue this process until the entire groove has been cut.

If using a router, choose a bit that is the width of the groove you want to cut. Use a rip fence or clamp a temporary guide in place and cut the groove with one pass of the router. You should move the router through the wood in the same direction that the bit is spinning. Most routers spin clockwise, so that means cutting from left to right.

Joining

After you've cut two pieces of wood, you'll bring them together to create a joint. Though there is a huge variety of possibilities, there are only four types of joints used in these projects: butt, miter, dado, and rabbet.

BUTT JOINTS

When two square cut pieces come together the result is a butt joint. Butt joints are used almost exclusively in these projects because they are the easiest to execute. Though butt joints have their strength and aesthetic limitations, most of these can be overcome with good design and proper finishing.

MITERED JOINTS

A mitered joint is created when two boards are mitered and brought together to form a 90-degree corner. A mitered joint brings together the ends of two pieces of wood, whereas a butt joint brings together the face of one board and the end of the

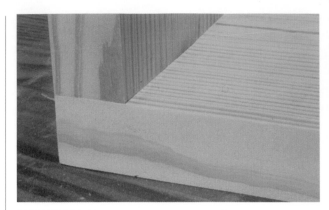

BUTT JOINT. **Here two square-cut pieces come together to form a corner.**

other. This end, or endgrain, of the board will often accept paint and stain differently than the faces of the wood, leaving an uneven finish. Because a mitered joint leaves only the faces of your boards for finishing, the results will be more even.

GROOVED JOINTS

Grooved joints are created when a board is inserted into a dado. These joints are very strong and can be quite elegant. I use them only in specific situations in these projects. For example in the medicine cabinet (page 50), I chose shelving that is too thin

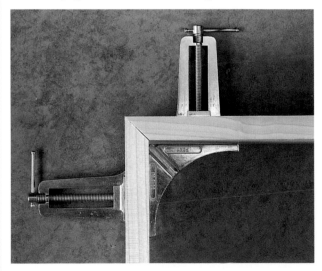

MITERED JOINT. **Here two pieces of wood with mitered ends are joined to form a corner. Notice how the end grain of both boards is hidden in the joining process. When executed cleanly, a mitered joint can be almost invisible.**

to be nailed or screwed, so I used a dado joint to hold the shelves in place. In the bathroom cabinet (page 117), I used a rabbeted joint to hide the back of the cabinet.

Fastening

After cutting and bringing two pieces of wood together, the last step in the joinery process is to securely fasten the joint. As is customary in this book, the fastening options are simple and straight-

DADO JOINT. **A board fitted into a three-sided rectangular groove is called a *dado joint*.**

RABBETED JOINT. **A board fitted into a two-sided rectangular groove cut along the edge of a one board is called a *rabbeted joint*.**

forward. For the most part, you'll join boards using glue, clamps, and screws, with the occasional nail thrown in as necessary.

CLAMPING

A nail or screw entering a joint can be pushed one way or the other by the grain of the wood, which, in turn, can cause the joint to move. The best way to avoid this problem is to securely clamp the joint together before adding fasteners. For basic butt joints, which include the vast majority of the joints in this book, a few bar clamps get the job done nicely. Mitered joints can be a pain to hold together with bar clamps alone. A good solution here is to use a corner clamp either alone or in combination with bar clamps. Corner clamps sit on your work surface and have two adjustable guides that pull the boards together, creating a corner when tightened.

GLUING

The ability to forgo fancy joinery is greatly enhanced by the powerful tool that is glue. When used in conjunction with clamping and screwing or nailing, glue

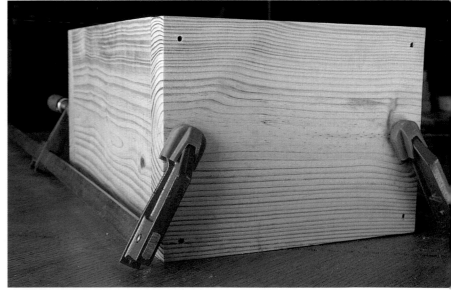

CLAMPING. **Clamps act as extra hands to hold joints in place until the glue dries or fasteners are applied.**

provides tighter, stronger joints. If you don't believe me, glue two pieces of white pine together with carpenter's glue, let the bond set overnight, then try to break them apart. Chances are you'll break the wood itself instead of the glued joint.

But glue does have its down sides. Because wood swells and shrinks as humidity levels change, locking joints in place often fights this natural movement. Where a nail or screw can give a bit to let a joint move, glue usually holds fast. As is always the case though, nature (i.e., the wood) wins. In the end the wood cracks to relieve the pressure created by the wood's natural movement. Wood moves mostly across the grain, so lumber glued face to face will expand less than lumber glued edge to edge. In any case, we're goal-oriented beginners, so we'll sacrifice a little perfection for convenience. By the way, plywood and other sheet materials aren't as susceptible to this expansion and shrinkage as lumber is, which is one reason they are used when a wide board is needed.

There are many varieties of glue, but I've always found just plain ol' interior carpenter's glue—often called yellow glue—to do a great job. Application is easy. First, make sure that any sawdust or dirt is removed, then just spread a thin bead of glue on both pieces of the joint and clamp them together. For most joints, you'll be able to release the clamps after ten to thirty minutes.

PREDRILLING

There are two ways to nail or screw a joint together. In the first, you hold the two boards together and just start nailing or screwing. This method can result in cracking or a misaligned joint. The better method is to prepare the joint by predrilling holes for the fasteners.

In one approach, you drill a hole in the outer board to allow the fastener shaft and threads but not the head to pass through. This clearance hole allows the shaft and threads of the fastener to hold the inner board,

PREDRILLING. **Predrilled holes prepare the wood for fasteners.**

while the head of the fastener holds the outer board. If using screws, some joints call for a second, or pilot, hole (see figure 3) in the inner board that is equal to the diameter of the screw's shaft. In some situations, you'll widen the top of a predrilled hole to make a bit more room for the fastener's head. This is called *countersinking* and the bit a *countersink bit*. For some joints you'll use a pilot hole, a clearance hole, and a countersink, for others you'll use only pilot and clearance holes, on a few you'll use only pilot holes, and still others you won't predrill at all. The diameter of the fastener, location of the joint on the board, and species of wood are some of the variables to take into account when deciding on a specific fastening strategy. As you get more experience, these decisions will become second nature. For now, though, I'll make specific suggestions as to when clearance or pilot holes should be used in the joints.

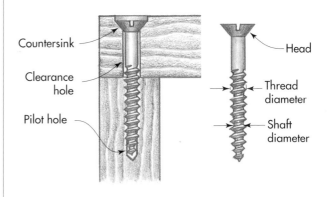

Countersink · Clearance hole · Pilot hole · Head · Thread diameter · Shaft diameter

Figure 3

Basic predrilling technique is simple. Set the drill to its fastest speed and drill holes so that the fastener will enter the middle of the joint's inner board. Make sure to bore parallel to the board's faces. Though it's nice to have a symmetrical fastener layout, adjust placement as necessary so that you aren't drilling through knots.

SCREWING

After gluing, clamping, and any necessary pre-drilling, you'll fasten most joints with screws. Square-drive screws in combination with a cordless drill and the correct driver are hard to beat for the beginning woodworker. The technique is simple. To give yourself more control, set your drill to a slow speed. Making sure that the driver is set securely in the screw's head, twist the screw into place just below the surface of the board with a light and steady pressure. If the screw starts to bind, let up on the trigger immediately. Put the drill in reverse, pull the screw back out, and investigate the problem. You may need a larger pilot hole or perhaps you are hitting a knot. In any case, a broken screw can be a real pain to get out, so don't be too aggressive. If you use softwoods, you're unlikely to experience this problem.

NAILING

As mentioned earlier, I prefer screws to nails in basic projects. The main reason is that screws can be removed and nails usually can't. That's a big help to the beginning woodworker who needs to be given room to make a few mistakes. Still, I do use nails on some joints, so let's go over basic nailing technique. First, you're building furniture, not framing a house. Though you might have a variety of hammers laying around already, the best tool for these projects is a finishing hammer, something with a small head that is light enough to be maneuvered in tight spots—a 13-ounce works well. In order to protect the surface of your project, take care to see that the head of your hammer never touches the wood when nailing. This is accomplished by driving the nail until the head is protruding about $1/16$ inch above the surface of your board. From here, drive the nail home with a thin piece of metal called a *nail set*. Nail sets come in a variety of sizes for setting different-size nails.

Sanding and Finishing

It might seem that once the joinery is completed, the project is almost finished. A little sanding and painting is all that's left. In fact, I estimate that sanding and finishing represented somewhere around half the time the two of us spent on the projects in this book. It's obvious, then, that this part of the process deserves full attention.

Sanding

For the most part, to sand or not is an aesthetic decision. But if you want your projects to look like the ones in this book, you'll have to sand them. Sanding, the process used to smooth the surfaces of the wood, is actually a form of cutting. The abrasive minerals on sandpaper are sharp and cut wood much like a saw blade. Sandpaper is labeled by the size of the abrasive mineral, or grit, that coats the cloth or paper backing. The smaller the number designating the paper, the larger the particle or grit.

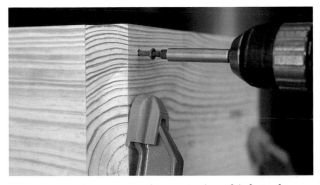

SCREWING. **Screws are inexpensive, high-tech machined components used to make strong precision joints with minimal work or skill.**

In other words, a 60-grit paper is covered in large, coarse abrasive, whereas as 150-grit paper is covered in a fine abrasive.

PREPARING TO SAND

Before sanding, you have to fill all fastener holes and any other imperfections in the wood. You can fill fastener holes either with wood putty or plugs. Plugs are small, rounded, tapered pieces of wood. If using plugs, your goal is to sink the fasteners just deep enough into the wood to allow the installed plug to protrude slightly above the face of the wood. Apply a bit of glue into the hole and push the plug into place. After the glue dries, you can sand the plug flush with the face of the wood.

The other option for filling fastener holes, or any other imperfection in the wood, is to use wood putty. As usual, there are a lot to choose from. Some putties are designed to work well with stains while others are for rebuilding damaged wood. The general-purpose putties are inexpensive, easy to apply, paint-able, and can be sanded soon after application. However, they sometimes don't work well with stains. Just be sure to read the label of the putty with your finishing technique in mind.

SANDING TECHNIQUE

After filling all holes and imperfections, you're ready to sand. The basic approach is to work the wood with a series of sandpaper grits from rough to fine. The general sanding regime is as follows. Start by inspecting all of your joints. Are there any places where wood is sticking out where it shouldn't be? If so, use a 60-grit paper to trim these spots to make the joints flush. Next, use 80- or 100-grit paper over the whole project. This should even any fluctuations in contour and take off any remaining bumps or quirks. At this point, check your puttying job and add putty where needed. For shallow holes, most putties will dry in 10 or 15 minutes. With the holes filled, continue sanding with 150-grit paper. This process should leave your surface very smooth without any noticeable transitions between joints. If you want an even finer surface, continue with a light sanding using 220-grit paper.

Some wood already has a nice surface when you buy it, so you can get by with less sanding. On most projects, I started with 80-grit paper and worked up to 150- or 220-grit for the final surface. General wisdom says to sand with the grain of the wood. That isn't always true, but it's a good rule of thumb. With my tool of choice, the random-orbit sander, sanding in one direction or another makes no difference.

Finishing

The finish of a piece of furniture is its final surface. In this book, that means paint, stain, or some kind of clear coat sealer. Why apply a finish at all? One reason is functional. The cell structure of wood isn't impervious to intrusion. I've already mentioned how wood can shrink and swell by taking on or giving off water. For the same reason, wood can stain if something is spilled on it. Wood can also simply absorb dirt and dust. Without finish, your pristinely sanded wood probably won't stay that way for long. A finish, however, can seal and protect your projects from damage. One advantage of wood's absorbency is that it accepts a wide variety of coatings. This means that wood can be transformed to fit many design concepts. I'll touch on a few basics to get you started. For more information, ask questions in the paint section of your building supply store, then just jump in.

The first step to a good finish is to clean off all of that sawdust created during sanding. You can do this with any clean soft rag or you can buy a tack cloth designed especially for the task. Next, choose the finish of your choice and apply it. One general piece of advice: try a chosen finish on a scrap of the wood used in your project before committing to coating your newly completed masterpiece. Regardless of what the color chip or the picture on the label looks like, you won't really know how your project will take a finish without testing.

PAINT

Painting is probably the most widely shared construction skill among the general populace. The reasons are twofold: (1) basic painting technique is easy to learn, and (2) painting has an amazing power to transform. If you don't believe me, change the color of your living room from white to fluorescent orange and watch the mood of your family transform instantly. For beginning woodworkers, painting also enables you to mask mistakes and imperfections.

Paint is basically colored pigment that has been mixed with a binder. In oil paints, the binder is some kind of oil, often linseed oil. Oil paints dry slowly which makes them easier to blend from light to dark in application, a trait that is useful in faux finishing. Another advantage of oil paints is that the depth of their color doesn't lessen during the drying process. A disadvantage of oil paints is that brushes need to be cleaned with mineral spirits. Latex paints, on the other hand, contain a synthetic binder. Because latex paints are water based, they dry very quickly through evaporation and can be cleaned up with warm water.

The surface to be painted is often prepared with a coat of sealing primer. Pine lumber can bleed sap which will stain your finish, but good sealing primers prevent, or at least minimize, the problem.

THE POWER OF FINISHING. **By simply changing the finish of a project, you can go a long way toward creating the aesthetic you want.**

Sealing primers also create a better surface to which paint can adhere and provide a uniform surface color which helps keep the finished color uniform.

Here are a few basic tips to improve your painting skills. Don't be penny wise and painting foolish by buying cheap brushes. A quality brush is a must if you want a smooth finish. If you clean them well and don't abuse them, good brushes can last a long time. You need just the right amount of paint on your brush, which takes a bit of practice. Mainly, it simply takes focusing on what you're doing and looking closely at the results. The basic concept is to build up the paint with a series of smooth, thin layers. Gravity will pull on paint applied on a vertical surface which can cause it to sag. That's why you'll achieve the smoothest finish by painting only on horizontal surfaces. That means painting a bit, waiting for that paint to dry, then turning the project and painting some more. This brings us to the most important painting skill: patience. It takes as long as it takes, case closed.

STAIN

Though there are opaque stains, the stains used on these projects have a level of transparency that allows the grain of the wood to be visible. I used stains, then, to change the color of the project while highlighting the character of the wood. The possible downside of this property for the beginner is that stains will show and possibly even highlight and exaggerate imperfections in your work. On the other hand, stains allow you to adjust the depth of the color. The more coats you apply, the deeper the color.

There are many options in the staining world. Water- or oil-based. Brush- or wipe-on. Opaque or semi-transparent. Some stains require a protective coating, others don't. Oil-based stains dry more slowly, giving you more time to create an even coat, especially on large surfaces. Water-based stains are easy to apply and come in a wider variety of colors. Gel stains have a thicker consistency and don't run as much during application. It takes a little experimenting to figure out which stains work best for you. Before staining, you may choose to apply a wood conditioner, which will help the wood take the stain more evenly. This is especially a good idea when using softwoods with an open grain. Take

STAINS. **There are a variety of types of stains available, each appropriate for a given set of situations.**

note that different conditioners are used with oil- and water-based stains.

My general staining technique is to apply the first coat quickly with a brush, then to apply subsequent coats with a rag. Rag application doesn't run as much and allows you to apply stain and soak it up in the same step, thus helping you get a more even coat.

CLEAR-COAT FINISHES

Whether painting, staining, or even if you want to keep the natural look of the wood, you may decide to use some sort of clear-coat sealer. These finishes, including varnishes and polyurethanes, can contain natural oils, such as linseed and tung oils, synthetic materials, or some combination of the two. Polyurethane is a common synthetic sealer used on floors and furniture. In addition to providing protection from water penetration and staining, sealing coats can bring out the wood grain and deepen its color. Sealers can be applied with a cloth or a brush, depending on the finish recipe. Light sanding is often required between coats, but each finish has unique characteristics and demands, so ask questions when you buy them. If all else fails, read the label.

NO FINISH

Wood is a beautiful, natural material that can be functional and appealing without any finish at all. Personally, there's nothing I like better than a solid old table with lots of chips, gouges, and cup stains to tell you the story of its life. If it fits your tastes, there is absolutely nothing wrong with leaving your projects unfinished.

■ GETTING STARTED

Now you're ready to start building. If you're a beginner, getting started can be a bit intimidating, so let's take a second to put things in perspective. This book is about storage, and at its core all storage is a box. My approach, then, is to teach you how to build a box, then show you different ways to embellish that box to make a huge variety of furniture that provides storage for various uses.

Each time you consider whether or not you want to tackle the challenge of a particular project, start by looking for the boxes inherent in the piece. There's always a core box. Often that box is divided into a number of other boxes by shelves. A drawer is just a box inside of slightly larger box. Once you learn to look at storage furniture from this perspective, it becomes less intimidating. I mean, if you can build one box, you can build them all, right?

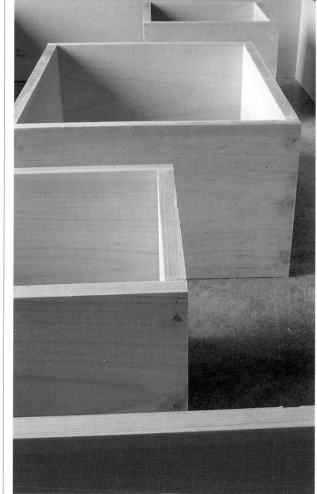

BUILDING BLOCKS. **Almost all storage units are, at their core, a box. For that reason, most of the projects in this book are really just embellished boxes.**

INEXPENSIVE ELEGANCE. **Beauty doesn't have to come with a big price tag. Here, a tinted oil-based stain brings out the grain in this inexpensive lauan plywood.**

At the same time, I don't want to be cavalier. In my opinion, building anything is hard work. It takes focus, precision, patience, and the ability to solve problems. If you're a beginner, you may have trouble jumping right into building the last few projects in this book. But that doesn't mean you have to build all of the projects in order. Just remember that if you come up against something that seems difficult in one project, chances are that it has been covered in more detail earlier in the book. Use earlier project instructions, photos, and, of course, the Basics chapter as a resource.

General Tips and Advice

Before diving into the projects, let's discuss a few specific situations you'll run into over and over in this book.

Ripping the Rounded Edges Off 2x Lumber

All 2x lumber at your local lumber yard has been shaped with rounded edges. These edges are a problem in furniture building because they make joints, especially my trusted pal the butt joint, look uneven. My solution is to rip ⅛ inch off both edges of all the 2x lumber used on the projects in this book. One method for accomplishing this is to use a circular saw outfitted with a rip fence. Simply clamp the board to your work surface, set the fence guide about ⅛ inch away from the blade, and rip the edge off each side of the board. Of course, if you have a table saw, this process is even easier.

Wall Mounting Options

A number of these projects need to be mounted on a wall. Others sit on the floor but, to keep them from tipping over, should also be secured to a wall. Of course, the best way to mount a project varies from one project to the next, but the basic instructions will be the same.

THE WALL

The first step is figuring out how the wall was built. If it's a wood-framed wall, chances are that the studs will be spaced 16 inches apart, though 24 inches is another possibility. Finding studs is an arcane art. You can rap your knuckle on the wall, listening and feeling for solid wood. You can measure over from known studs, such as those at windows or electrical outlets. Or, you can go high-tech and buy an electronic stud finder. Once you're close, use a small finish nail to poke holes through the wall surface to find the stud.

If your wall is masonry, then the whole wall is the structural system, so no scavenger hunt is needed.

But, as in life, there's no free lunch. To attach anything to a masonry wall, you'll need to drill a hole into the wall. Drilling into masonry may call for a more powerful drill than the small cordless models I've recommended for these projects.

THE HARDWARE

Most of the hanging projects in this book are designed to be mounted with screws driven directly through the back of the project into the structural system of the wall. If you choose not to go that route, there are many options. For lighter projects, you can get away with the old picture hanging stand by: a loop of strong wire on the back of the project hung on a nail or screw securely fastened to the wall. Beyond that, you'll find a huge array of mounting hardware at your local building supply store. These range from simple hooks or serrated bars that grab fasteners protruding from the wall to fancier two-part units that attach both to the project and the wall and then interlock. The coolest specimen of this variety that I've used has a little built-in level.

The important thing about picking hardware is making sure that it is strong enough for the specific situation at hand, i.e., the combination of your wall and the given project. If you have any doubts about mounting, ask someone to help you. This isn't an area for experimentation.

Drawer Options

Quite a few of these projects have drawers in them. Though they can be complicated, I've kept the drawer designs for projects simple and well within the reach of the beginning woodworker. That said, there's no slumming here. If you look at older furniture, you won't find a ball bearing or metal track anywhere, yet the drawers open and close just fine.

I use several drawer designs. The simplest is just a box set inside a slightly larger box. The step up is a drawer with sides slightly wider than the back and the drawer bottom set higher than the bottom of the

sides. This design reduces friction because the actual drawer bottom doesn't touch the case; only the sides of the drawer do. The cream of the drawer crop for this book is the reduced-friction drawer combined with a closure block that makes it impossible to pull the drawer all the way out. Though I've chosen drawers that work well for each project, you can use any of the drawer designs for any given project. For example, if you're afraid of accidentally pulling the wine rack drawer all the way out and spilling everything on the floor, add a closure block like the one used on the kitchen cart (page 129).

Adjusting the Projects to Fit Your Needs

One very good reason for building your own furniture, or doing anything yourself for that matter, is to get exactly what you want. It may turn out that a particular project is perfect for your needs. On the other hand, it might be that the piece needs just a small adjustment to make it work for you. I encourage you to look at the place where you plan on using a given project and consider adjusting dimensions to fit your needs. For example, the rolling cart (page 41) is designed so that six of them can fill the space under both sides of a queen-size bed. If you are looking to fill the space under a double or king-size bed, it's easy to adjust the length of the cart to fit your situation.

Don't Just Follow the Instructions

Woodworking is all about proportions. That's one reason why building projects from books can be problematic. If you deviate from a measurement by a small amount, let's say $\frac{1}{16}$ inch or even less, then the rest of the written measurements in the instructions may not work for you. These small differences can accrue from cut to cut and eventually make a mess of things. If you want your projects to come out as clean as the finished photos in this book, then start with my measurements. But if your first measurements are a little off, adjust later cuts to see that the project goes together square. Sometimes the easiest way to do this is to mark board lengths directly off other similar parts or off partially assembled projects.

PROJECTS

Nested Tables

Since all storage is basically a box, start your storage journey by simply building a couple of boxes. Without embellishments to worry about, you can put your focus on accurate measuring and making clean cuts that are straight and square. These are skills you'll need on every other project. But don't get me wrong, this isn't a training exercise. By adding feet and a nice finish, your simple boxes become versatile nested tables. At our house, we flank our couch with a pair of nested tables at each end. The big one holds a reading lamp and the smaller one is used for magazine storage and is pulled out to serve as a footstool. But these same tables could be put to use anywhere. Make several sets and play with various finishes to match different rooms in your house.

Part	Qty.	Material	Dimensions
Top and base of small box	2	2x10 pine	12 inches long
Sides of small box	2	2x10 pine	15 inches long
Top and base of big box	2	2x12 pine	18 inches long
Sides of big box	2	2x12 pine	22 inches long
Feet	8	2x2 pine	2 inches long

Nested Tables Plans

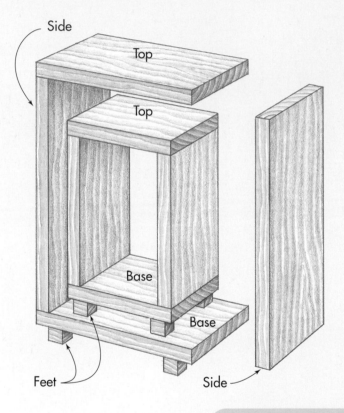

FINISHED DIMENSIONS
18" x 11¼" x 26½"

Tools

Measuring tape

Circular saw or miter saw

Cordless drill with drivers and bits

Speed square or combination square

Framing square

4 bar clamps, at least 24 inches long

Rubber mallet

Random orbital-orbit sander with discs from 60 to 220 grit

Eye and ear protection

Fasteners

24 square-drive deck screws, 2½ inches long

16 finish screws, 2¼ inches long

Glue

Notes on Materials

I used southern yellow pine for this project because it is easy to work with, strong, inexpensive, and widely available at any lumber yard where we live. However, any lumber available as a 2x12 will work.

Instructions

A cardinal rule of efficient woodworking is to do similar tasks at the same time. This simple practice saves a lot of time and effort. With that in mind, notice how we treat the construction of these two boxes as a single project, building them both simultaneously so that we finish one group of similar tasks before moving on to the next.

1 Using a table saw or a circular saw outfitted with a rip fence, rip the rounded edges off the 2x10 and 2x12 lumber. Cut the tops, bases, and sides of both boxes to length. As you measure each piece, inspect the lumber around the area to be cut. Since screwing into a knot can cause the wood to split, try to avoid having a knot at the end of any pieceboard.

2 Clamp together the top and base of the smaller box. Using the appropriate drill bit for the width of your deck screws, drill clearance holes through each end of the clamped boards as described on page 26 in the Basics chapter (see photo A.) If your drill bit isn't long enough to drill completely through both boards, remove the clamps and finish drilling the holes in the bottom board. Now repeat this process with the top and base of the larger box.

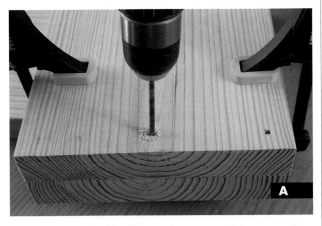

CLEARANCE HOLES. **Clamp the top and bottom of each box together and drill clearance holes appropriate for the diameter of your deck screws.**

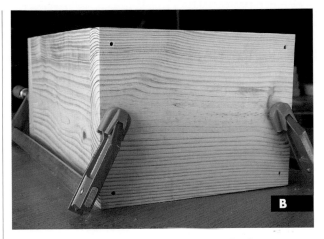

CLAMPING TO CHECK THE FIT. **Clamp the box together temporarily to check that your joints are tight, or at least close enough that a little work with clamps and a mallet will make them so. Use a framing square to make sure that the box is square before committing to screws and glue.**

3 To assemble the boxes, first clamp the small box together to check the fit (see photo B). If the base or top is cupped (see figure 2 page 11 in Basics), place the top of the cup toward the interior of the box. This will make it easier to flatten the board with the clamps. Check to make sure the box is square by setting a carpenter's framing square against the outside corner. Throughout the length of the top and sides, there shouldn't be any gap between the square and the box.

If everything looks good, remove the clamps, apply glue, and then clamp the box together again. Screw in all three deck screws for one joint before moving on to the next. Make sure to sink the screw below the surface of the board by about 1/16 inch. Drive one of the outside screws first, then the middle, and finally the second outside screw, adjusting the fit as necessary with a mallet as you go. This technique allows you to correct small deformities in your lumber to create tight joints. If you are using very soft wood or the joint requires a really good wallop with a hammer, place a scrap of wood, called a *beater board*, over the spot you plan to hit. Striking the

Nested Tables

beater board instead of your project will prevent the hammer from denting your lumber. Now repeat step 3 to assemble the pieces of the bigger box.

4 To make the feet, start by sanding a 3-foot-long piece of 2x2. Cut the feet to length from this board. Drill two clearance holes to match your finish screws through each leg. After applying glue, use the finish screws to attach a foot at each corner of the two boxes—1 inch from the end and ½ inch from the front or back edge (see photo C).

ATTACHING THE FEET. **Make sure to hold each leg firmly in place as you attach it with finish screws.**

5 Working on both boxes at the same time, fill screw holes and imperfections in the joints with a wood filler that fits your chosen finish, then sand all of the surfaces. (For information on wood filler and sanding, see page 28 in Basics.) If an end isn't completely flush with a side at any of your joints, a random-orbit sander with 60-grit paper will quickly fix the problem. If your joints are perfect and you only need to smooth the wood, start with 100-grit paper, then move up to 150 grit. If you want a really fine surface, finish up with 220 grit.

6 Wipe off all sawdust with a tack cloth, then finish both tables as desired. The project pictured here was first covered with a coat of primer, then sanded with 220-grit paper. Finally several coats of semi-gloss latex paint were applied.

Rolling Cart

In this project, you lay down your basic box, add a bottom, a handle, some wheels, and a little decorative trim to create a rolling cart. The only new skill you may need to learn is how to rip plywood. We designed this cart with under-bed storage in mind. Two of them can fit under the width of a queen-size bed, allowing access from both sides. A group of six will completely fill the under-bed space, creating a veritable storage oasis. However, by changing a few dimensions, this project can be easily adapted to solve other home-storage problems. For example, a smaller cart could be used in a closet for holding shoes or cleaning supplies.

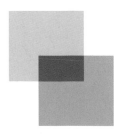

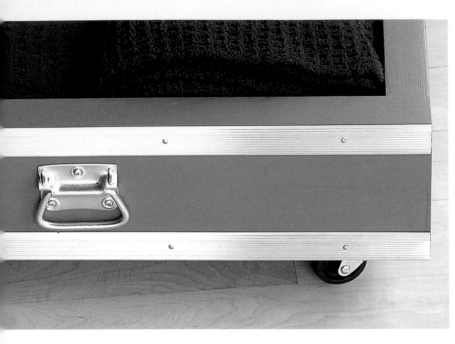

Tools

Measuring tape

Circular or miter saw

Cordless drill with drivers and bits

Speed square or combination square

2 bar clamps, at least 36 inches long

Tin snips or hacksaw

Random-orbit sander with discs from 80 to 220 grit

Eye and ear protection

Tin snips

Optional Tools

Table saw

Parts List

Part	Qty.	Material	Dimensions
Bottom	1	¾-inch plywood	24 x 30 inches
Sides	2	2x6 pine	27 inches long
Front and back	2	2x6 pine	24 inches long
Handle	1	collapsible utility handle	not wider than 3 inches
Trim	2	aluminum saddle threshold	24 inches long
Casters	4	plastic wheels	2-inch diameter

Rolling Cart Plans

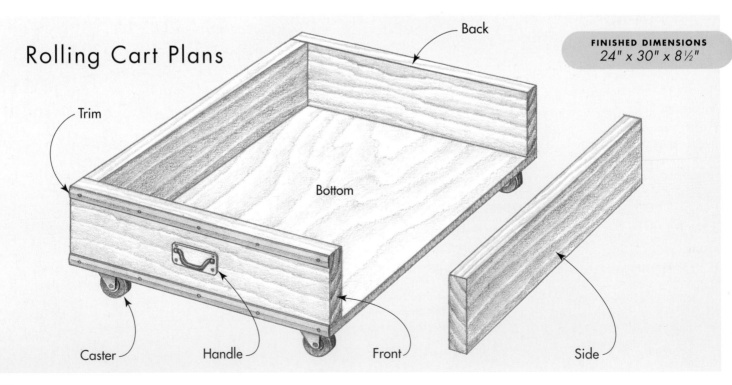

Back

Trim

Bottom

Caster

Handle

Front

Side

FINISHED DIMENSIONS
24" x 30" x 8½"

Fasteners

12 square-drive deck screws, 3 inches long

22 square-drive deck screws, 1⅞ inches long

10 finish screws, 1½ inches long

16 wood screws, ⅝ inches long

Glue

Notes on Materials

For an industrial look, I used a collapsible utility handle and trimmed the box front with an aluminum saddle threshold. Saddles are typically used to cover transitions between floor materials, such as where carpet meets tile. You should be able to find several different styles in the flooring area of your local building supply store. However, there is nothing magical about this material for this application. Any piece of metal or wood of the same width could create a similar effect. As for casters, I recommend plastic wheels because they are easier on flooring materials.

Instructions

Words of wisdom: you can cut a piece of wood shorter, but you can't make it longer.

This obvious fact forces all us carpenters and furniture makers to be very careful cutters. When building projects like the ones in this book, remember that your goal isn't to cut pieces to the exact length noted, but to cut a number of pieces to corresponding sizes that fit together square and flush to one another. With that in mind, when possible, decide what part is the size template for a project, then carefully match the rest of the pieces to fit that part. Using this technique takes a lot of pressure off your poor little measuring tape. In our rolling cart, the template is the plywood bottom. Its exact size after

cutting determines the exact length of the box sides, front, and back. Instead of measuring the length of the sides, front and back, mark them directly off the bottom of the box.

1 Cut the plywood bottom to size using a circular saw or table saw (see page 23 in Basics for plywood cutting options).

2 Using a table saw or a circular saw outfitted with a rip fence, rip the rounded edges off your 2x6 lumber. Next, cut the sides, front, and back to length. Based on the Parts List, you'll need two pieces 24 inches long and two pieces 27 inches long. In the real world, these pieces need to come together to make a box that fits exactly on top of the plywood bottom you've just made, so you should cut them to fit. If, for example, you bought a precut quarter-sheet of plywood, it will most likely be 23⅞ inches wide instead of the full 24 inches. Based on the true size of your plywood, cut the pieces of your box just a hair long and assemble them with clamps on top of the plywood and check the fit. Remember, you can always make boards shorter, but you can't make them any longer—don't be afraid to go back to the saw several times to get the length just right.

3 To assemble the box, first drill three clearance holes for 3-inch deck screws at each end of the front and back. Referring to the plans, glue, clamp, and screw the front, back, and sides of the box together.

4 Sand the inside of the box and the good side of the plywood bottom with 150-grit paper. Sanding now is a good idea because it will be difficult to sand those areas where the box meets the bottom after the project is assembled.

Rolling Cart

5 To attach the bottom to the box, start by drilling clearance holes for 1⅜-inch deck screws every 5 inches around the perimeter of your plywood bottom. These holes should be set ¾ inches in from the edges of the plywood. Set the box on a level work surface and place the plywood on top of the box so that the sanded side faces down. Line up the plywood with one of the long sides of the box and then screw it down using 1⅜-inch deck screws. Your box will most likely be out of square with the plywood. If so, place a clamp from corner to corner across one of the sides of the project. Set one end of the clamp on the box and the other on the plywood, then tighten the clamp to pull the box square to the plywood, as shown in photos A and B. With the clamp in place, screw the other three sides of the plywood to the box using 1⅜-inch deck screws.

6 Fill imperfections with wood putty and sand the cart as described in the Basics chapter. Wipe off all sawdust with a tack cloth and finish the project as desired. The sample project pictured here was first covered with a coat of primer, then sanded with 220-grit paper. Finally several coats of flat latex paint were applied.

7 After your finish has dried, center the handle on the front face of the box and attach it using the instructions that came with it.

8 Since you may have adjusted the size of the box slightly, measure the length of the front and cut lengths of the aluminum saddle threshold to fit your box exactly. Using tin snips is the easiest way to cut the aluminum threshold. Install one trim piece flush with the top and the other flush with the bottom of the front face of the box, using the finish screws.

9 Turn the box over and place a caster 1 inch in from each corner (see photo C). Attach the casters, using ⅝-inch-long wood screws.

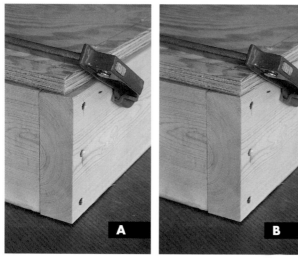

SQUARE THE BOX TO THE PLYWOOD. **If you've cut your plywood accurately, it will be square. Since your box isn't rigid, it will almost certainly be a bit out of square. After screwing one long side of the plywood bottom (to the side of the box), attach a clamp across the other side (A). With one end of the clamp set on the box and the other on the plywood, pull the box flush with the plywood (B) before installing the rest of the screws.**

ATTACH THE CASTERS. **Plastic casters are easier on most floor materials, especially wood floors. Attach a caster 1 inch in from each corner of the box. Notice the sloppy puttying job on the screw hole near the caster—because this is the bottom of the box and will never be seen, there's no reason to waste time on a quest for perfection.**

CD Rack

If you look closely at this project, you'll see that at its core it's very similar to the last project, the rolling cart: a simple box with a back. Yet, by using different lumber, adding shelves and attaching some creative trim, I've transformed the cart into a funky and fun CD storage rack. The movable dividers are a nice design addition, which allows you to organize your CDs into sections. These dividers double as structural support for the shelves, but there's no need to nail them in place. If you've built either of the first two projects, you shouldn't have any trouble completing this one.

CD Rack Plans

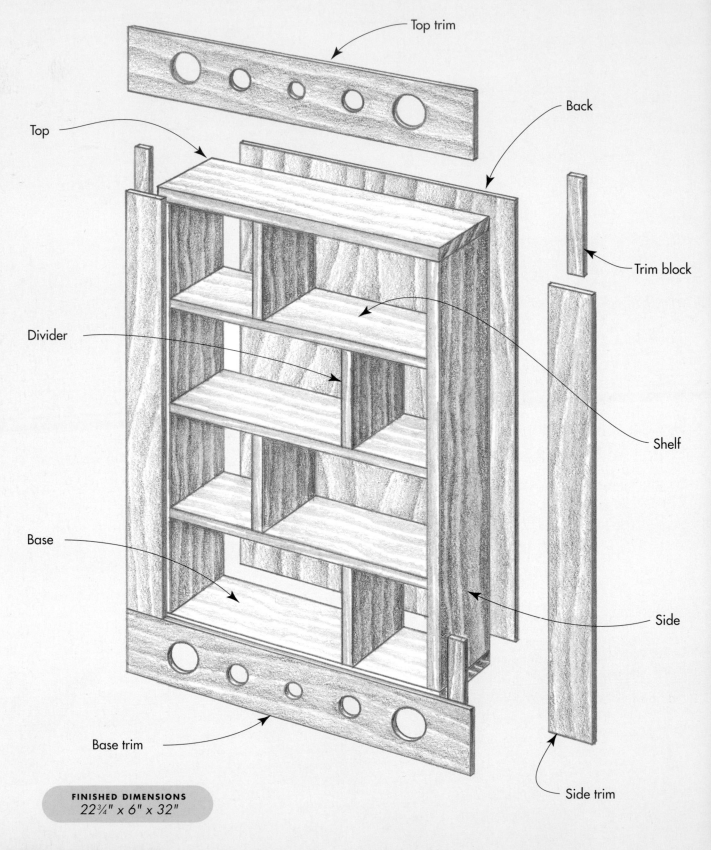

Top trim

Top

Back

Trim block

Divider

Shelf

Base

Side

Base trim

Side trim

FINISHED DIMENSIONS
22¾" x 6" x 32"

Parts List

Part	Qty.	Material	Dimensions
Top	1	1x6 pine	19 inches long
Base	1	1x6 pine	19 inches long
Sides	2	1x6 pine	23 ½ inches long
Back	1	¼-inch lauan plywood	19 x 25 inches
Shelves	3	½ x 6 cabinet grade pine	17 ½ inches long
Dividers	4	½ x 6 cabinet grade pine	5 ½ inches long
Top trim	1	¼-inch lauan plywood	4 x 22 ¾ inches long
Base trim	1	¼-inch lauan plywood	4 x 22 ¾ inches
Side trim	2	¼-inch lauan plywood	2 ⅞ x 24 inches
Trim blocks	4	¼-inch lauan	1 x 5 inches
Wall mounting hardware		any style	

Tools

- Measuring tape
- Circular saw or miter saw
- Cordless drill with drivers and bits
- Speed square or combination square
- 2 bar clamps, at least 36 inches long
- 2–8 small spring clamps
- Random-orbit sander with discs from 80 to 220 grit
- Eye and ear protection

Optional Tools

- Table saw
- Hand plane
- Hole saw kit

Fasteners

- 30 finish screws, 1⅝ inches long
- 40 3d finish nails
- Glue

Notes on Materials

For this project, I chose cabinet grade pine. Cabinet grade lumber is selected for its clean grain and absence of knots and other imperfections. For more on lumber selection, see page 10 in the Basics chapter.

Notes on Technique

A hole saw is a round saw blade that is mounted on a drill to cut a hole of a given diameter. Hole saw kits contain a variety of these blades. Such kits can be expensive, but there are very reasonable economy models available. I used such an inexpensive kit to cut the holes in our trim. However, these holes are decorative and can be easily omitted if you don't have a hole saw kit. Other decorative options could be attaching found objects, such as old bolts, or pieces of wood to the trim. For example, different size square pieces of 1x stock could be attached in a pattern to create a similar effect to the holes I cut.

Instructions

The best measuring device is a physical object. If there are consistent spaces between any elements in a project, then cut pieces of plywood, lumber, or whatever scrap you have around to act as spacers during installation. In this project, I was able to use the movable dividers that were already part of the design as spacers for the shelf installation.

1 Cut the top, base, and sides of the box to size. Drill three clearance holes at each end of the top and base to accommodate your finish screws. Glue and clamp the box together with the top and base, capping the sides as shown in the plans. Drill pilot holes through each clearance hole and then screw the box together with 1⅞-inch finish screws.

2 Fill any imperfections in the joints or lumber on the interior of the box and sand as described on page 28 of the Basics chapter. It's much easier to fill and sand now, before the back and shelves are installed.

USING SPACERS. **Here, the first shelf has been installed and the second shelf is in place on top of the spacers. This is a quicker, more accurate way to evenly space shelves. It also makes installation easier because it helps hold the shelf in place while screwing. (Note: The spacers seen here were cut a bit long so that they would show up well in the photo. You'll be using the dividers for the project as spacers, so they'll be flush with the front face of the box.)**

3 Cut the plywood back. Since your project may vary slightly from the printed dimensions, measure the actual length and width off your box and cut the plywood back for an exact match.

4 Lay the box face down on your worktable, apply glue, and place the plywood back on top of the box. Using 3d nails, attach one side of the plywood to the box, then square the back to the box with clamps using the same technique as described in the rolling cart project on page 44. Place the rest of the nails carefully so that they don't end up pushing out the side of the wood. If, after all of this careful work, your plywood still ends up protruding past the box slightly on one side or the other, use a hand plane to trim it flush.

5 Measure the interior dimension between the two sides at the bottom of the box. Cut three shelves to this length out of the ½-inch pine. These need to fit snugly, so cut carefully. Next, cut your dividers.

6 With the box lying so that it's plywood back rests on your work surface, place a divider in each corner of the bottom of the box. Apply glue to the ends of a shelf and slide it into the box snug against the top of the dividers. Using a speed or combination square, draw a faint line on both sides of the box at the place where the middle of the shelf rests. Drill three pilot holes through each of these lines into each end of the shelf. Pushing the shelf against the divider, attach the shelf to the sides of the box with finish screws. Pull out the dividers, place them on top of the shelf you've just installed, and install the next shelf using the same method. Do the same for the third shelf (see photo A).

7 To make sure that the shelves aren't sagging, place a divider between each shelf in the middle of the box. Then turn the box over and use a straightedge to continue the pencil lines, marking the shelf locations onto the plywood back (see photo B). Nail four evenly spaced 3d nails through each of these three lines, into the back of the shelves.

ATTACHING THE BACK TO THE SHELVES. **To secure the back, mark out the nail locations by extending the pencil lines from the sides of the box.**

8 Cut the four pieces of trim and the trim blocks. (Note: since the trim is too thin to be connected with nails or screws, glue small cleats—I call them *trim blocks*—across each joint to hold the trim box together.) Set the trim face down on your work surface so that it forms a box as illustrated in the plans. Apply a bit of glue to the side trim pieces where they intersect, then apply glue to the trim blocks and clamp them in place with spring clamps (see photo C). Push each corner tightly together for a few seconds after the spring clamps are in place. (If you only have two spring clamps, glue one corner at a time.) If desired, drill holes with hole saws in the top and base trim in an arrangement that suits your taste.

9 To install the trim box, lay the CD rack flat on its back on your worktable. Apply glue and set the trim box in place. Position the trim so that an equal amount of the face of the CD rack is exposed on all four sides. Attach each side of the trim box to the CD rack with 3d finish nails spaced every 5 inches.

10 After removing the dividers, fill all the screw holes and any imperfections on the exterior of the box. Sand the exterior as described on page 28 of the Basics chapter, then lightly sand the trim box with 220-grit paper. Wipe off all of the sawdust with a tack cloth, then finish the rack and dividers as desired. The sample project pictured above was covered with several coats of an oil-base burnt orange stain.

Notes on Installation

Choose wall-mounting hardware appropriate for your particular installation (see page 32 for mounting options). To properly support the unit, make sure to attach the mounting hardware through the back of the box into one of the shelves

ASSEMBLING THE TRIM BOX. **After applying glue, clamp the trim blocks in place so they straddle each corner joint. Place the trim blocks on the back of the trim box, about ¾ inch from the inside.**

Medicine Cabinet

In the last project, the CD rack, shelves were added to a basic box. In this project, I add a door to the box or shelf package. I also had some fun with the design and created a shelf that is accessible without opening the door. This all adds up to an introduction to several new skills: cutting miters, preparing a basic dado joint, cutting a rectangle out of the middle of a sheet material, and installing simple hinges. After the sawdust clears, the result will be a sleek, contemporary medicine cabinet with a unique look.

Medicine Cabinet Plans

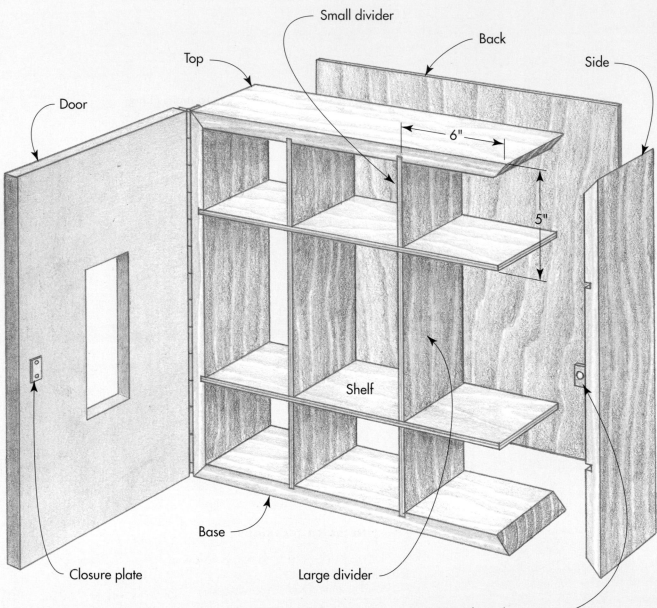

Small divider

Back

Top

Side

Door

6"

5"

Closure plate

Shelf

Base

Large divider

Magnetic door closure

FINISHED DIMENSIONS
18" x 6¼" x 18"

Parts List

Part	Qty.	Material	Dimensions
Top	1	1x6 poplar	18 inches long
Base	1	1x6 poplar	18 inches long
Sides	2	1x6 poplar	18 inches long
Back	1	¼-inch lauan plywood	18 x 18 inches
Shelves	2	¼x6 poplar	17 inches long; cut to fit
Large dividers	2	¼x6 poplar	8 inches long; cut to fit
Small dividers	4	¼x6 poplar	4¼ inches long; cut to fit
Door	1	½-inch MDF or high-grade plywood	18 x 18 inches
Continuous (piano) hinge	1		1-inch wide x at least 16 inches long
Magnetic door closure	1		

Tools

Measuring tape

Circular saw or miter saw

Jigsaw

Cordless drill with drivers and bits

Speed square or combination square

2 bar clamps, at least 24 inches long

1–4 corner clamps

Random-orbit sander with discs from 80 to 220 grit

Eye and ear protection

Optional Tools

Table saw

Hand plane

Hacksaw or metal blade for circular saw

Fasteners

28 finish screws, 1⅞ inches long

Screws appropriate for your chosen hinge

Glue

Notes on Materials

For this project I used poplar for the box and shelving because it takes paint very nicely. However, any smoothly milled, kiln-dried lumber would work. I chose medium density fiberboard (MDF) for the door. MDF is a sheet material made of wood particles glued together. MDF is inexpensive, very smooth, and unlikely to warp, making it perfect for a small door. Alternately, you could use any high-grade plywood with at least one smooth face. I chose a continuous (or piano) hinge for the project both because it's easy to install and it has the industrial look that complements our chosen finish. Piano hinges come in a variety of lengths. Sixteen inches is perfect for this project, but if you can't find that length, get a longer one and cut it with a hacksaw.

Notes on Techniques

I decided to miter-cut the joints of our box for a more uniform look. If you don't have an electric miter saw, butt joints will work fine. If you use butt joints, I recommend painting the cabinet to cover the end grain. Even then, you may see a bit of end grain through the paint on your finished project.

Instructions

The thinner the wood, the harder it is to attach it using fasteners such as screws or nails. One solution is to use more complicated joinery techniques, such as the dadoes used to join the shelves and dividers to the box itself. Where structural support is needed, dado joints are a good choice. And glue alone is all that is needed to attach the vertical dividers.

1 Cut the top, base, and sides of the box. If you decide to miter your joints, cut a 45-degree miter at each end of each of the four pieces of the box. (See page 24 of Basics for a description of miter cuts.) Each piece should be 18 inches from the long point of one miter cut to the other. (If you choose to use butt joints instead, square the end of each piece. The top and the bottom should be 18 inches long and the sides 16½ inches long.)

2 Using the dimensions illustrated in the plans, cut two dadoes into the inside faces of the top, bottom, and sides of the box. For more on cutting dadoes, refer to page 22 of the Basics chapter. (Note: if you have chosen to use butt joints, the outside of each dado on your side pieces will be 4¼ inches instead of 5 inches from each end of the board.) Measure your shelving boards and mill dadoes sized to fit the thickness of the boards. Cut each dado about ¼ inch deep, and make sure that your shelving boards fit snugly within the grooves (see photo A).

3 Before assembling your box, drill three clearance holes ⅜ inch from each end of both the top and bottom of your box. Glue and clamp the box together. Drill a pilot hole through each clearance hole and then screw the box together with 1⅝-inch finish screws. Mitered boxes can be difficult to clamp. I suggest using a corner clamp to hold the base of each corner together (see photo B). This will get your joints in the ballpark of being flush. Make small adjustments as you predrill each hole so that the joint is flush at the place you are drilling.

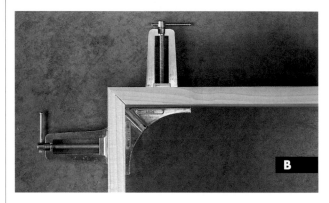

CORNER CLAMP. **Mitered joints can be difficult to hold with bar clamps. One solution is to use a corner clamp to hold the bottom of each joint tightly in place while adjusting the top of the joint with your hands as you drill pilot holes and attach screws.**

4 Cut the shelves. These cuts need to be very accurate, so don't trust the dimensions in the Parts List. First, measure the exact distance between the bottom of the dadoes opposite each other on the sides of your box. Then, cut the two shelves to fit snugly and slide them into the dadoes on the side of the box. Remember that it's better to cut the shelves a bit long and have to trim them than it is to discard boards cut too short.

5 To make finishing easier, remove the shelves and sand their surfaces and the interior of the box with 150-grit sandpaper. Apply a small amount of glue onto the ends of the shelves and slide them in place.

NOT TOO LOOSE, NOT TOO SNUG. **The shelves and dividers need to fit snugly into the dadoes. The groove should be only a hair wider than the shelves and dividers so they can slide easily into place.**

6 Measure the distance between the two shelves where they intersect a side of the box. Cut the large dividers to this length and sand them with 150-grit sandpaper. Use a square to transfer the location of the dadoes on the top and bottom of the box onto the front edges of the shelves. Next, wrap your pencil lines onto the top and bottom faces of the shelves so that you can see where the dividers are supposed to go. Apply glue between the lines on the shelves and to the ends of the large dividers themselves. Slide the large dividers into place and clamp them up (see photo C).

7 Measure and cut the small dividers to fit, then sand them with 150-grit paper. Test fit all four small dividers, then glue and clamp them in place between the lines you've drawn on the shelves. Make sure that the ends of the small dividers line up with the ends of the large dividers, as if the pieces were one long board.

8 Measure the outside dimensions of your box. Cut a piece of ¼-inch lauan plywood to these exact dimensions. This will be the back of your cabinet. To make the door of your cabinet, cut a piece of MDF or finish plywood to these same dimensions.

9 Make sure the table is clean of all debris so that you don't mar the face of the door, then set the door face down on your worktable. Place the cabinet on top of the door and check to see that all edges of the door and cabinet are perfectly aligned. With a sharp pencil, trace the interior box defined by the inside surfaces of the shelves and the large dividers onto the door. Clamp the door to your worktable with a smooth piece of scrap under it. Using a spade bit, drill a ⅜-inch hole, slightly inset, on each corner of the box you drew. Take care to let up on your drilling pressure as the bit nears the back of the cut. If not, you'll push roughly through the face of the MDF rather than cutting it cleanly (see photo D). Install a fine-cutting wood blade in

INSTALL THE LARGE DIVIDERS. **After transferring the placement of the dadoes in the top and base of the box to the shelves with pencil lines, apply glue between these lines and to the top and bottom of the large dividers, then clamp the dividers into place between the shelves.**

your jigsaw, set the blade through one of the holes, and then carefully cut out each side of the box, taking the line as you cut. (*Taking the line* means to actually cut the pencil line rather than cutting on one side of it.)

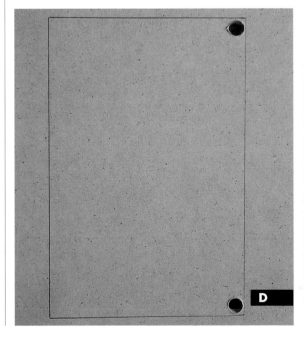

CUT THE HOLE IN THE DOOR. **Drill holes into each corner of the box you've marked out in the middle of your door. These access holes enable you to start the jigsaw cut and allow for easy transitions between the cuts for each side.**

Medicine Cabinet

10 To attach the back, drill four clearance holes on all four sides of the back for finish screws, set ⅜ inch from the edges. Sand the interior face of the back with 150-grit paper, then apply glue and attach the back to the cabinet with finish screws.

11 Fill holes and imperfections in the cabinet and door using a wood putty appropriate to your chosen finish. Sand the exterior of the cabinet (and both sides of the door if necessary) with 150- and 220-grit paper. Wipe off all sawdust with a tack cloth, then finish the cabinet and door as desired. The project pictured here was painted with a coat of primer, sanded with 220-grit paper, then covered with two coats of high-gloss enamel paint.

12 After the finish has dried, install the door and chosen closure. If you found a 16-inch piano hinge, great. If not, cut your longer hinge to length with a hacksaw or metal blade on your circular saw. Attach one side of the hinge to the edge of your door. The placement of the other side of the hinge will depend on the kind of magnetic door closure that you use. If your closure is designed to pull the door tight against the cabinet, attach the other side of the hinge to the cabinet so that there is no space between cabinet and door (see photo E). Some closures (the spring-loaded variety, for example) hold the door slightly out from the cabinet in the closed position. If you have such a closure, the hinge should hold the door the same distance away from the cabinet.

13 Choose wall-mounting hardware appropriate for your particular installation (see page 32 for mounting options).

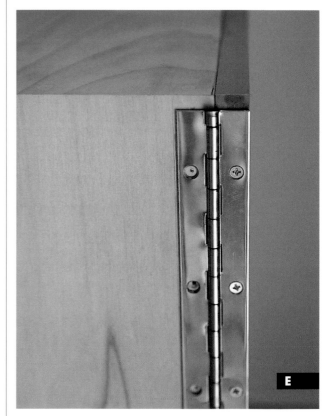

E

SECURE THE HINGE. **The hinge's position should be based on the type of door closure you've chosen. This continuous hinge is placed for a door closure that holds the door tightly against the cabinet.**

Mantle Shelf

Have you ever been in houses constructed 50 or more years ago? It seems like even modest homes built in those days have wonderful little touches—niches, arched transitions between rooms, or interesting trim. It's rare to find such details built into houses today, so we have to create our own. This project takes our basic box and transforms it into a stately mantle, simply by adding a bit of trim and a few precut wooden brackets. In this project you'll learn basic crown molding installation. Though crown molding can get complicated, this project has only two outside corners and two butt cuts. That's about the easiest crown molding installation you'll ever find, so it's a great beginner's introduction to this popular material.

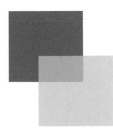

Mantle Shelf Plans

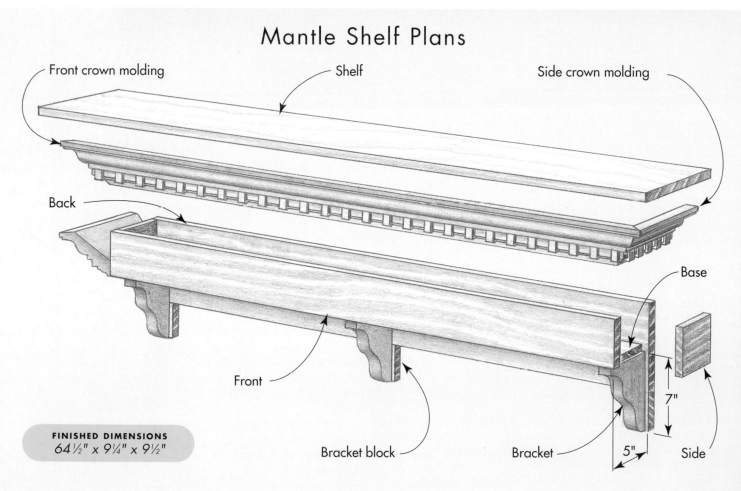

Front crown molding

Shelf

Side crown molding

Back

Base

Front

FINISHED DIMENSIONS
64½" x 9¼" x 9½"

Bracket block

Bracket

7"

5"

Side

Parts List

Part	Qty.	Material	Dimensions
Back	1	1x8 pine	55 inches long
Sides	2	1x4 pine	4⅜ inches long
Front	1	1x4 pine	55 inches long
Base	1	1x6 pine	ripped to 4⅜ inches wide x 53½ inches long
Brackets	3	carved wood	see Notes on Materials
Bracket blocks	3	1x4 pine	ripped and cut to fit
Shelf	1	1x10 pine	64½ inches long
Front crown molding	1	see Notes on Materials	cut to fit
Side crown molding	2	see Notes on Materials	cut to fit

Tools

Measuring tape

Powered miter saw, circular saw, or hand miter box and backsaw

Cordless drill with drivers and bits

Speed square or combination square

2 bar clamps, at least 12 inches long

Random-orbit sander with discs from 80 to 220 grit

Eye and ear protection

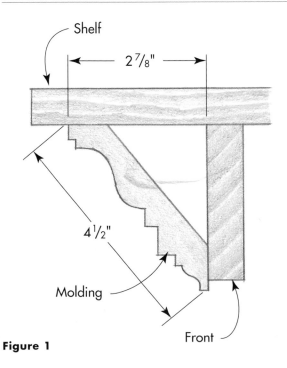

Figure 1

Fasteners

70 finish screws, 1⅜ inches long

Glue

Notes on Materials

There are many crown molding patterns to choose from. The one I picked for this project is from a group called *dentil*. You don't need to choose the same pattern. What's important is that your molding has close to the same installed dimensions (see figure 1) as mine. This is easy to check with a framing square, so take yours with you when you go to buy lumber. Easier still, take this book, show it to a salesperson, and tell them you want a molding with the same dimensions as illustrated.

Looking at the plans, you can see that I chose decorative brackets that are 5 inches wide horizontally and 7 inches long vertically. Each bracket is 2¼ inch wide. Your brackets can vary, but, for structural reasons, they should be between 4 and 5 inches wide horizontally. If they are more or less than 7 inches long vertically, simply adjust the bracket blocks to fit accordingly.

Instructions

Some finishes show imperfections, others hide them; therefore, the chosen final finish for a project determines how careful you need to be about details such as screw placement. Since we chose to finish this project with a stain, I was careful to place the visible screw holes symmetrically and evenly spaced. I also chose a putty designed to take stain. By the same token, I spent no time worrying about placement of the screw holes on the back of the box that would face the wall because they will never be seen. All attachments in this project are made using 1⅞-inch-long finish screws.

1 Cut the back, sides, and front of the box to size. Drill clearance holes and then glue and clamp your box together so that the sides are sandwiched between the back and front, as shown in the plans. Predrill through the clearance holes, then screw the box together.

2 Cut and rip the base piece. Using a straightedge, draw a line along the back piece between the two sides of the box. As shown in the

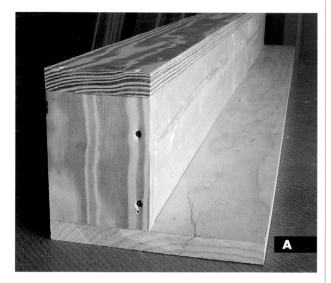

THE BASIC BOX. **Set the base flush with the bottom of the box and screw it in place. At this point, the shelf hasn't been installed, providing access to the interior of the box, so that the top of the brackets can be attached with glue.**

plans, apply glue and clamp the base of the box in place so that it is flush with the front, sides, and this pencil line. Predrill and attach the base with screws. Use two screws on each side and five screws on the front and back (see photo A).

3 Measure over 27½ inches from either end of the base and draw a line through the width of the board. This line is the exact center of the box. Center a wooden bracket on this line with the 5-inch side resting on the base and the 7-inch side resting on the back. Apply glue, predrill, and attach the bracket with two screws through the back. Make sure that your screws are entering the center of the bracket. Place the other two brackets flush with each end of the box and attach them in the same way.

4 To make the bracket blocks, measure the distance from the bottom of the back of the box to the bottom of the brackets. Rip down about 7 inches of 1x4 to this dimension. (Tip: if you use a circular saw with a rip fence instead of a table saw to make this rip cut, start with a much longer piece of 1x4 and clamp one end to your worktable.) Measure the width of the back of the bracket and cut three pieces of the ripped 1x4 to this dimension. Referring to the plans, apply glue, predrill through the blocks, and screw them to the bottom of the brackets. Important note: make sure that the bases of the brackets are thick enough to accommodate the 1⅞-inch finish screws. If not, use a shorter screw.

5 Cut the shelf. Draw a pencil line 4¾ inches in from each of its ends. Referring to the plans, apply glue and clamp the shelf in place so that its back is flush with the back of the box. The lines you've drawn will sit on the outer edge of each side of the box. Predrill and screw the shelf into place. Use two screws on each side and five screws on the front and back of the box. Since it would be difficult to do so after the crown molding is installed, sand the base of the box and the bottom of the shelf now with 100- and 150-grit paper. Also, examine the joint between both sides and the front of the box. If anything isn't flush, sand with 60-grit paper to make it so.

Now it's time to cut and install the crown molding. Though the process isn't complicated, cutting crown molding can be confusing if you haven't done it before. Crown molding can be expensive, so if you have any scrap crown, try a few practice cuts first.

6 Start with a 65 inch long piece of crown molding. Set the molding in your hand or powered miter saw with the bottom against the fence as shown in figure 2. Set the saw to 45 degrees to make cut #1 illustrated in figure 3. While holding the board firmly in place, cut the miter.

7 Set the box with the shelf side down on your worktable. Referring to the plans, clamp the cut end of the molding to the left side of the box so that the back edge of the cut sits flush with the end of the box. Make sure that one side of the molding is sitting flat on the underside of the shelf and the other is sitting flat on the front of the box, overhanging it slightly to create a reveal, as illustrated in figure 1.

Clamp the molding tightly to the other end of the box and make a pencil line on the back of the molding where it is flush with the front of the box. Place the molding back in the miter saw in the same orientation as before and set the saw to 45 degrees in the opposite direction to make cut #2 as shown in figure 3. It will be difficult to determine exactly where to make the cut, so just be sure to cut the board long on this pass, about 1 inch past the pencil mark you've drawn. You'll now be able to judge the relationship of the saw to the line better, so make the cut again. I suggest leaving this cut a bit long also and then checking your board by clamping it to the box again. After you've got the cut just right, clamp the molding in place against the front of the box.

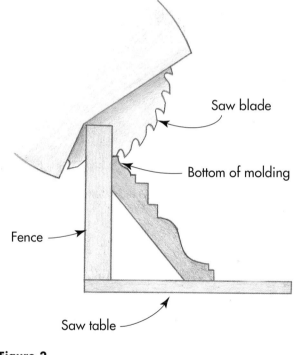

Saw blade

Bottom of molding

Fence

Saw table

Figure 2

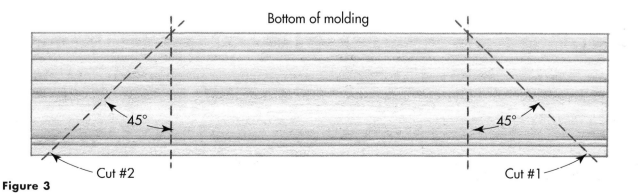

Bottom of molding

45°

45°

Cut #2

Cut #1

Figure 3

INSTALLING THE FRONT MOLDING. **After carefully cutting the molding pieces and testing the fit, attach the front molding. The bottom of the molding should overhang the box slightly while the shelf should overhang the top of the molding.**

8 Next, cut two pieces of molding 6½ inches long. Cut one piece with the saw set for cut #1 and the other for cut #2 (see figure 3 on page 61). Test-fit these pieces at each end of the molding that is clamped in place to make sure that the joint will be tight. If everything looks good, unclamp the front molding, apply glue and reclamp. Predrill holes along the bottom and top of the molding. Drill at an angle so that the screws will enter both the shelf and face. Drill five evenly spaced holes in the top and bottom of the molding. Use a countersink bit on each predrilled hole to make space for the heads of the screws. This will help prevent cracking in your carefully cut molding (see photo B).

9 Set one piece of side molding in place and scribe a line along its back where it is flush with the back of the box. Make a square cut along this line. Go through the same process for the other piece of side molding. Apply glue and install these pieces with the same method used on the front molding (see photo C).

10 Fill holes and imperfections in the top of the shelf and sand with 100- and 150-grit paper. Wipe off all sawdust with a tack cloth, then finish the project as desired. The sample project pictured here was covered with several coats of a water-based antique red stain.

Notes on Installation

This project is designed to be mounted by screwing directly through the back piece into the structural members of a wall. Drill two pilot holes through the back into each wall member, then screw the shelf to the wall. Once installed, fill the screw holes with wood putty and touch up your finish. Alternatively, there are a variety of hanging hardware choices that could be mounted on the back of the box that would allow you to leave your finish untouched. See page 32 for general comments on wall mounting options.

INSTALLING THE SIDE MOLDING. **After cutting them to length, install each piece of side molding.**

Mirrored Shelf with Drawers

The front entryway is often overlooked as a storage zone, but it shouldn't be. You need a place to hang your keys, hats, and umbrellas, as well as store gloves and put letters that need to be mailed.

It's also nice to have a mirror, so you can give yourself one final perusal before you head out into the world. By lengthening the back of our basic box to accommodate a mirror, adding some dividers and two simple drawers, We've created a versatile storage unit that can serve all of these purposes.

Mirrored Shelf Plans

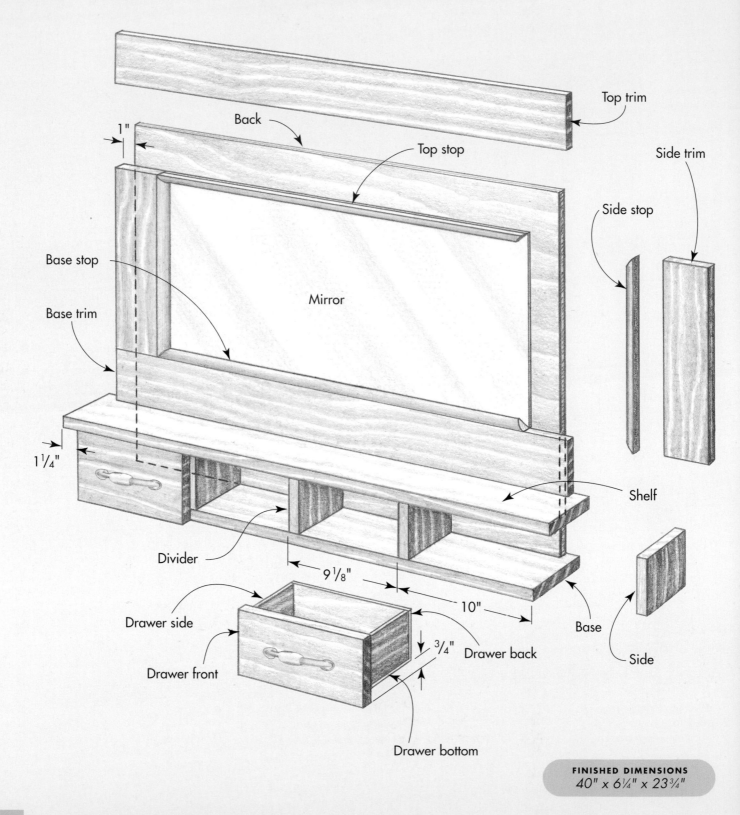

Top trim

Back

Top stop

Side trim

1"

Side stop

Base stop

Base trim

Mirror

Shelf

1¼"

Divider

9⅛"

10"

Base

Drawer side

¾" Drawer back

Side

Drawer front

Drawer bottom

FINISHED DIMENSIONS
40" x 6¼" x 23¾"

Parts List

Part	Qty.	Material	Dimensions
Back	1	¾-inch plywood	36 x 22 inches
Base	1	1x6 pine	ripped to 4¾ inches wide x 37½ inches long
Sides	2	1x4 pine	4¾ inches long
Shelf	1	1x6 pine	40 inches long
Dividers	3	1x4 pine	4 inches long
Top trim	1	1x4 pine	38 inches long
Base trim	1	1x4 pine	38 inches long
Side trim	2	1x4 pine	12 inches long
Mirror	1	⅛-inch custom cut mirror	30¾ x 11¾ inches
Top stop	1	see Notes on Materials	31 inches long
Base stop	1	see Notes on Materials	31 inches long
Side stops	2	see Notes on Materials	12 inches long
Drawer sides	4	1x4 pine	ripped to 3⅛ inches wide x 3⅝ inches long
Drawer backs	2	¼-inch lauan plywood	8¼ x 3⅛ inches
Drawer bottoms	2	¼-inch lauan plywood	8¼ x 3⅞ inches
Drawer fronts	2	1x6 pine	ripped to 4³⁄₁₆ inches wide x 10 inches long
Drawer handles	2	any style	
Decorative hooks (optional)	6	any style	

Tools

- Measuring tape
- Circular saw or miter saw
- Cordless drill with drivers and bits
- Speed square or combination square
- 2 bar clamps, at least 48 inches long
- Random-orbit sander with discs from 80 to 220 grit
- Eye and ear protection

Fasteners

- 48 finish screws, 1⅝ inches long
- 30 finish nails, 1¼ inches long
- 14 finish nails, 1 inch long
- Glue

Notes on Materials

The mirror stop in the Parts List will be used to hold the mirror in place, but you won't find any lumber labeled mirror stop at your local hardware store. I bought a ⅜ x 1¼-inch door stop and ripped it down to ⅝ inch wide. Any wood that is ½ inch (or less) thick and 1 inch (or less) wide will work. As for the mirror, you can have it cut to size at a glass supply store, but some home centers will cut mirrors as well. The drawers in this project are very small and are designed to be pulled completely out of the case—they're really more like small storage boxes than drawers. For that reason, I chose handles instead of drawer pulls. The handles make it easier to hold the little boxes while fishing around inside them.

Instructions

Remember that woodworking is all about proportions. Look, for example, at the dividers in this project. The measurements given were arrived at by evenly spacing the dividers within the box after it was made. I didn't start with given numbers, but deduced them from measuring the actual project at the appropriate stage. The same goes for the drawer dimensions. If you want this project to come out as clean as the finished photo of the sample, take measurements off the project you're actually building instead of relying solely on the Parts List. In this project, all screwed connections are made using 1⅝-inch-long finish screws.

1 Cut the back, base, and sides of the box to size. Lay the back of your box flat on your worktable, then apply glue and clamp the sides and base to the back. Make sure that the base laps over the bottom of the back and the sides lap over the sides of the back. Drill pilot holes and assemble the box using screws.

2 Cut the shelf to size and draw pencil lines across the width of the board 1¼ inch in from each end. Apply glue and clamp the shelf in place so that these pencil lines are flush with the outside edge of the sides (see photo A). Drill two pilot holes per side and attach the shelf with screws.

3 Cut the dividers from a length of 1x4, then install them in the box. To accommodate the screws, pre-drill two holes through the shelf and base for each divider.

4 Cut your trim pieces to length. With the project laid flat on its back on your worktable, apply glue and clamp the trim into place. Notice that the installed trim should create a box that extends 1 inch past the plywood back on the top and both sides (see photo B). Nail these pieces to the plywood back using 1¼-inch finish nails. Locate the nails in pairs, with the first nail placed about 1 inch in from the inside edge of the board and the second nail about 1½ inches in from the other side. Use three sets of two nails on the sides and four sets of two nails along the top and base.

TRIM OVERHANG. **The trim runs 1 inch past the plywood back on the sides and top. Because this piece will be mounted on a wall, a 1-inch overhang is enough to hide the end grain of the plywood back.**

PLACING THE SHELF. **The shelf overhangs the box 1¼ inches on both sides.**

5 Cut the mirror stops to length with a miter cut at each end. The dimensions in the Parts List are measured long point to long point for these miter cuts, but it's a good idea to measure your actual project and cut your pieces for a precise fit. Set your mirror in place, then apply glue and install the mirror stops as seen in the plans. Use 1-inch finish nails and carefully predrill at an angle so that the nails will enter the side trim and avoid the mirror. Use four nails along the top and base and three nails along each side.

6 Cut all drawer pieces to size. Assemble the drawers by first attaching the sides to the back and then attaching the bottom to the sides. Use glue and two finish screws for each joint. Next, draw a pencil line along the entire length of each drawer front ¾ inch in from one edge. Set a drawer on a front so that the bottom of the drawer sits on this line. Adjust the drawer so that the sides are evenly inset from each end of the front, then scribe a line along the sides of the drawer onto the back of the front. Apply glue and clamp the drawer into place along these lines. Predrill two holes into each side of the drawer and attach the front with finish screws. Repeat this process for the other drawer (see photo C).

7 Prepare your drawers for the handles that you've chosen. For most handles this will entail drilling clearance holes for two screws that will then be pushed through the front of the drawer from the inside and screwed into the handles. But don't install the handles yet—wait until the finish has been applied.

8 Fill holes and imperfections with a wood filler appropriate to your chosen finish, then sand all of the surfaces as described on page 28 of Basics. Wipe off all sawdust with a tack cloth, then finish the project as desired. The sample project pictured here was first covered with a coat of primer, then sanded with 220-grit paper, and finally coated with several coats of a matte latex paint.

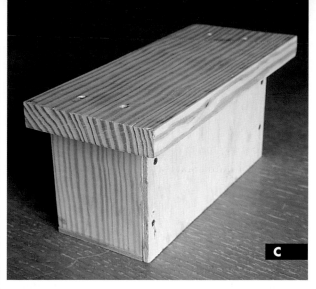

BASIC DRAWERS. **The small, simple drawers for this project are more like removable storage boxes. They are a great introduction to drawer construction for the beginner.**

9 Once the finish has dried, install your drawer handles. If desired, install decorative hooks as a final touch. Hooks on side trim could be used to hold keys. Hooks on the box sides could hold coats and umbrellas.

10 There are a variety of ways this project can be mounted on a wall. The simplest is to hang it like a picture with wire and picture hooks. Another option is to screw the trim around the mirror into structural wall members. This would require drilling pilot holes and touching up your finish after installation. For more information on wall mounting, see page 32.

Storage Bench

There's a lot of wasted space in your house. For example, under every chair and sofa there's a nice empty spot inhabited only by dust bunnies. Why not use it for storage?

In this project, I've done just that by combining a bench with a shelf unit. This design is easy to build—it's simply a big, long box built strong enough to sit on. It has the same elements as previous projects, such as a shelf and dividers, just on a larger scale. I gave this one a rustic finish, but the sleek, square angles of this project can accommodate a variety of tastes by simply changing the finish style. This bench works great by the front door as a place to put on, take off, or store your shoes.

Storage Bench Plans

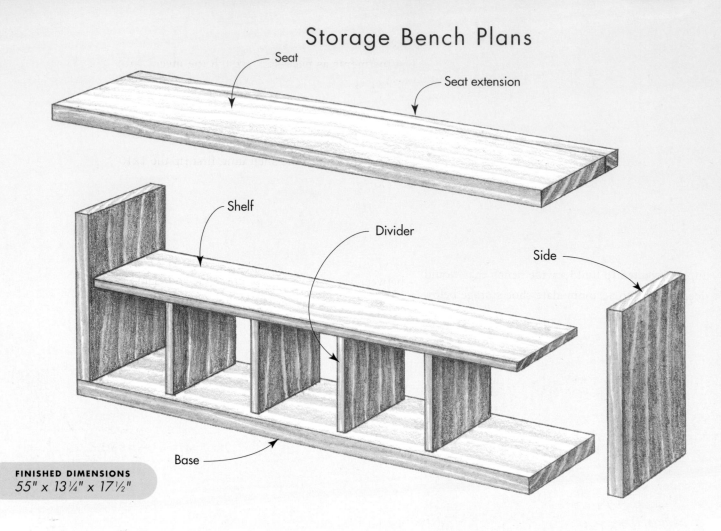

Seat

Seat extension

Shelf

Divider

Side

Base

FINISHED DIMENSIONS
55" x 13¼" x 17½"

Parts List

Part	Qty.	Material	Dimensions
Base	1	2x10 pine	51 inches long
Sides	2	2x10 pine	16 inches long
Seat	1	2x12 pine	55 inches long
Shelf	1	1x10 pine	48 inches long; ripped to 8¾ inches wide
Dividers	4	1x10 pine	9 inches long, ripped to 8¾ inches wide
Seat extension	1	2x4 pine	55 inches long; ripped to 2 inches wide

Tools

Measuring tape

Circular saw or miter saw

Cordless drill with drivers and bits

Speed square or combination square

Framing square

4 bar clamps, at least 24 inches long

Rubber mallet

Random-orbit sander with pads from 80 to 220 grit

Eye and ear protection

Optional Tools

Table saw

Fasteners

16 square-drive deck screws, 3 inches long

12 square-drive finish screws, 2¼ inches long

18 square-drive deck screws, 2½ inches long

Glue

Instructions

Mass-produced materials have their advantages, but they can be confining, as well. Take this project for example. I wanted to build a wide bench that would be deep enough to accommodate shoe storage below the seat. However, the widest lumber commonly found at lumber yards is 11¼ inches—not enough to accommodate most shoes (or at least mine). I deepened the bench by edge-gluing and screwing an extra 2-inch-wide board to the rear side of our bench's seat. This is a basic glue-up common in furniture making, and it's a technique we'll use more extensively in later projects in the book.

1 Rip the rounded edges off both sides of your 2x10 and 2x12 lumber. Then cut the seat, base, and sides of your box to length.

2 To assemble the basic box, first drill three clearance holes for 3-inch deck screws 2¼ inches from each end of the seat. Next, drill three holes of the same size ¾ inch from each end of the base. Now, mark a pencil line through the width of your seat 2 inches in from each end. Referring to the plans, glue and clamp the box together so that the base and sides are flush. Place the seat so that it is flush with the sides at the back and the outer edge of the sides resting on the pencil lines you drew on the seat. This will create a 2-inch overhang at the ends and front of the seat. Drill pilot holes through all clearance holes (see page 26 for a description of pilot holes). Check to see that all the joints are flush and use a framing square to make sure

that the box is square. Use your mallet to make adjustments as necessary. Attach the pieces with 3-inch deck screws.

3 Sand the interior of the box, starting with 60- or 80-grit sandpaper and move up to 150 grit.

4 To make the shelf unit, first rip the 1x10 lumber to 8¾ inches wide and cut the shelf and dividers to length from this ripped board. Then make pencil lines on the shelf to locate the dividers so that they give you five equally spaced cubbyholes. Drill three clearance holes for your finish screws between each set of lines. Apply glue and clamp the dividers in place between the lines. Drill pilot holes through the clearance holes and attach the dividers using 2¼-inch finish screws (see photo A).

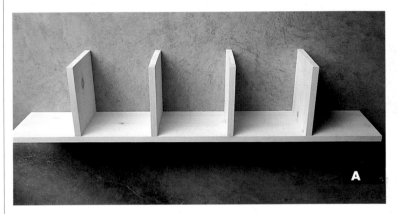

SHELF UNIT. **Attach the dividers to the shelf first, then install this unit in the bench.**

5 To attach the shelf unit to the bench, mark pencil lines on the base to locate the dividers, just as you did on the shelf. Drill three clearance holes for 2½-inch deck screws between each set of lines. Then, drill three clearance holes for 2½-inch deck screws through both sides of the box—10⅞ inches up from the bottom of the base. At this point, go ahead and set the shelf unit into place. The bottom of the shelf should intersect each side 9 inches up from the top of the base of the box. One side of the shelf unit should be flush with the back of the base and sides of the box, creating a reveal between the shelving and the box at the front of the bench (see photo B). Drill pilot holes through the clearance holes on both sides and attach the shelf board with 2½-inch deck screws. Now, lay the bench on its back and clamp the dividers in place so that they sit between the lines you've drawn on the base. Drill pilot holes through the clearance holes in the base and attach the dividers using 2½-inch deck screws.

CREATING A SHADOWLINE. **By ripping down the shelving and dividers to 8¾ inches, a reveal is created between the shelving unit and the box itself. This little detail adds visual interest to this simple project, but it also allows you to be a bit less careful in your installation—there's no need to worry about creating a perfectly flush joint.**

6 To make the seat extension, first cut a 51-inch length of 2x4. Rip the rounded edge off one side then rip the board to 2 inches wide. Drill four evenly spaced clearance holes for 3-inch deck screws through the middle of the thicker portion of

this board. Apply glue and clamp this piece to the back side of the seat so that it is flush with the back of the box. Drill pilot holes through the clearance holes and attach this piece with 3-inch deck screws (see photo C). You now have a 13-inch-wide seat for your bench.

SEAT EXTENSION. **Attach the 2-inch-wide seat extension to the back side of the seat. This creates a wider seat than would be possible using off-the-shelf framing lumber.**

7 Fill any holes and imperfections with wood putty appropriate to your chosen finish. Sand the outside of the bench, starting with 60- or 80-grit paper; finish with 150- or 220-grit. Pay particular attention to the joint on the seat of the bench seat where we added the 2 inches of width. If you fill and sand this joint carefully, you won't be able to tell that the seat isn't a single board. This is where your random-orbit sander will really earn its keep.

8 Wipe off all sawdust with a tack cloth, then finish the bench as desired. The sample project pictured here was washed with several coats of a satin latex paint. Washing is a simple technique which involves brushing paint on then wiping some of it off. The paint soaks into the wood, but does not completely obscure the grain. By wiping some areas more than others, you can make the furniture look as if it were painted long ago and the color has faded with time.

Bookshelf

Bookshelves are nothing more than a big box organized into smaller boxes. (Good news, since you should be getting pretty good at building boxes by now.) Unfortunately, bookshelves are often boring pieces of furniture. What's worse, they often have uniform shelf spacing so that they can only hold a very limited array of book sizes. In this project, I've solved both problems by creating a fun shelf layout designed to accommodate books of various dimensions. The relatively short height of this design makes it the perfect replacement for a bedside table. Of course, there are many other places around the house where this bookshelf will come in handy.

Bookshelf Plans

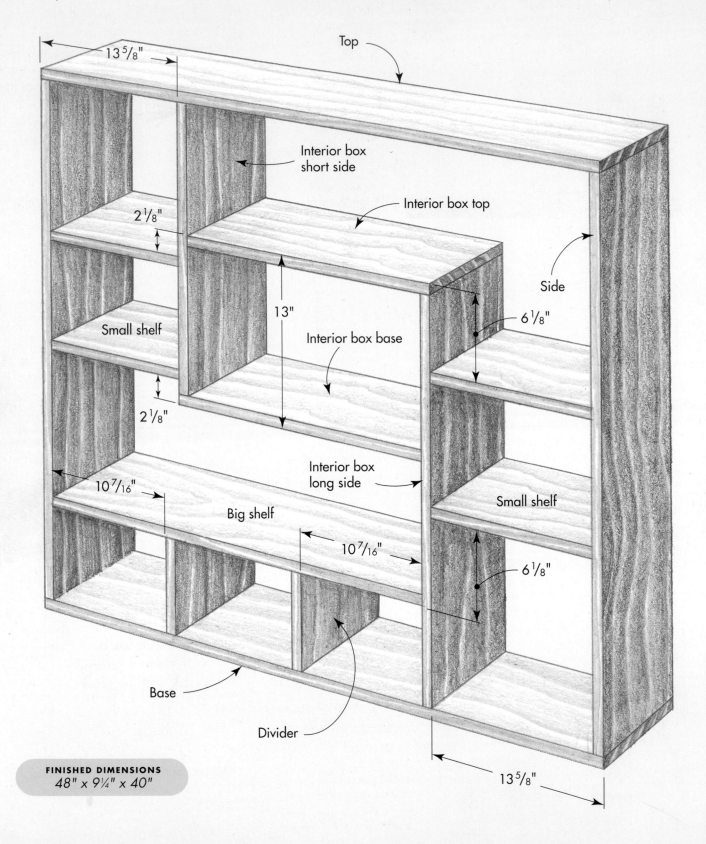

Top

$13^5/_8$"

Interior box short side

Interior box top

$2^1/_8$"

Side

Small shelf

13"

$6^1/_8$"

Interior box base

$2^1/_8$"

Interior box long side

$10^7/_{16}$"

Big shelf

Small shelf

$10^7/_{16}$"

$6^1/_8$"

Base

Divider

FINISHED DIMENSIONS
48" x 9¼" x 40"

$13^5/_8$"

Parts List

Part	Qty.	Material	Dimensions
Top	1	1x10 pine	48 inches long
Base	1	1x10 pine	48 inches long
Sides	2	1x10 pine	38½ inches long
Interior box top	1	1x10 pine	20 inches long
Interior box base	1	1x10 pine	20 inches long
Interior box short side	1	1x10 pine	22 inches long
Interior box long side	1	1x10 pine	28 inches long
Big shelf	1	1x10 pine	32⅞ inches long
Dividers	2	1x10 pine	7 inches long
Small shelves	4	1x10 pine	12⅞ inches long

Tools

Measuring tape

Circular saw or miter saw

Cordless drill with drivers and bits

Speed square or combination square

Framing square

4 bar clamps, at least 48 inches long

Rubber mallet

Random-orbit sander with pads from 80 to 220 grit

Eye and ear protection

Fasteners

75 square drive finish screws, 2¼ inches long

Glue

Instructions

Notice that in this project, I saved time by only drilling clearance holes through joints at the ends of boards. The soft white pine I used could easily have split here. However, in the middle of the board where most of the shelving is attached, there is little chance of splitting. Unless otherwise specified, use three 2¼-inch finish screws to attach each joint.

1 To assemble the basic box, first cut the top, base, and sides to length. Pre-drill three clearance holes for your finish screws ⅜ inch in from each end of the top and base. Then glue and clamp the four sides of the box together. If you are using a very soft wood, like the white pine used here, there is no need to drill pilot holes—simply screw the box together.

2 It's easiest to assemble the interior box as a single unit, then install it into the larger box. Start by cutting the four pieces of the interior box unit to length. Predrill clearance holes ⅜ inch in from one end of the top and base. Glue, clamp, and screw the top to the long side and the base to the short side.

Bookshelf

A

INTERIOR BOX UNIT. **Assemble the interior box so that the distance from the outside of the top to the outside of the base is 13 inches at both sides.**

Then join these two L-shaped components together to create the interior box—the outside dimension between the top and base should be 13 inches (see photo A). In addition to measuring, use a carpenter's square to make sure that the interior box is in fact square before screwing.

3 To attach the interior box, first lay the main box onto your work surface, then glue and clamp the interior unit to the main box as shown in the plans. This is a place where following instructions

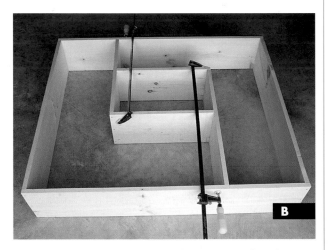

B

TWO BOXES. **Attach the two boxes together being careful that the sides of the interior box are square with the top and base of the main box.**

to the letter can get you into trouble. The important thing to remember is that the sides of the interior box need to be perpendicular to the top and base of the main box. Use a framing square to make sure this is true. If it isn't, then your box deviates slightly from our printed dimensions. That's fine—simply adjust the interior box unit so that it is square and screw it in place (see photo B).

4 Cut the big shelf and dividers to length. Glue, clamp, and screw the dividers to the shelf using the dimensions provided in the plans. (Note: remember that if you had to adjust the placement of your interior box, you'll need to adjust the printed measurements given here to fit your project. In that case, place your dividers by dividing the length of the big shelf by 3. Measure this distance in from each end of the big shelf and draw a line. Center a divider directly over each line.) Attach this unit to the main box as illustrated in the drawing. To insure consistent spacing, cut a 7-inch-long piece of scrap and use it as a spacer under each end of the big shelf as you screw it into place. Use a speed square to check that both dividers are square with the main box base before attaching them with screws.

5 Cut the small shelves to length. Glue and clamp them in place using the dimensions provided in the plans. Make sure that the sides of each shelf are square to the main box and the interior box, then screw them into place.

6 Fill holes and imperfections with a wood putty appropriate for your chosen finish. Sand all surfaces starting with 60- or 80-grit paper and finish with 150 or 220 grit.

7 Wipe off all sawdust with a tack cloth, then finish the bookshelf as desired. The sample project pictured here was first covered with a coat of primer, then sanded with 220-grit paper. Finally several coats of semi-gloss latex paint were applied.

Big Bookshelf

In this project, the concept of the box as storage is taken to new heights by connecting four boxes together with shelving and dividers. The result is a piece of furniture that is functional but also sculptural.

The wide variety of spaces between shelves makes this project equally suitable for books or as a display case for pottery and other artwork. It can also serve as a room divider, and, because of its structural nature, it looks great in that capacity even with nothing in it.

Big Bookshelf Plans

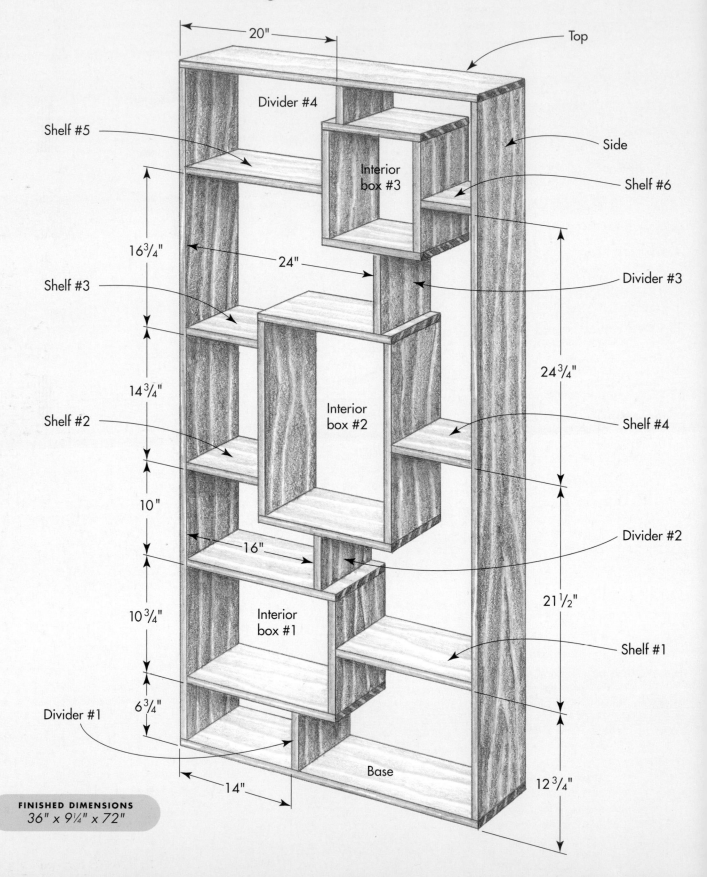

20"

Top

Divider #4

Shelf #5

Side

Interior box #3

Shelf #6

16³/₄"

24"

Divider #3

Shelf #3

24³/₄"

14³/₄"

Interior box #2

Shelf #4

Shelf #2

Divider #2

10"

16"

10³/₄"

Interior box #1

21¹/₂"

Shelf #1

Divider #1

6³/₄"

14"

Base

12³/₄"

FINISHED DIMENSIONS
36" x 9¹/₄" x 72"

Parts List

Part	Qty.	Material	Dimensions
Top of main box	1	1x10 pine	36 inches long
Base of main box	1	1x10 pine	36 inches long
Sides of main box	2	1x10 pine	70½ inches long
Top of interior box #1	1	1x10 pine	18 inches long
Base of interior box #1	1	1x10 pine	18 inches long
Side of interior box#1	1	1x10 pine	10 inches long
Top of interior box #2	1	1x10 pine	16 inches long
Base of interior box #2	1	1x10 pine	16 inches long
Sides of interior box #2	2	1x10 pine	20 inches long
Top of interior box #3	1	1x10 pine	12 inches long
Base of interior box #3	1	1x10 pine	12 inches long
Sides of interior box #3	2	1x10 pine	10½ inches long
Divider #1	1	1x10 pine	6 inches long
Divider #2	1	1x10 pine	5½ inches long
Divider #3	1	1x10 pine	8 inches long
Divider #4	1	1x10 pine	cut to fit
Shelf #1	1	1x10 pine	16½ inches long
Shelf #2	1	1x10 pine	9¼ inches long
Shelf #3	1	1x10 pine	9¼ inches long
Shelf #4	1	1x10 pine	9¼ inches long
Shelf #5	1	1x10 pine	16⅞ inches long
Shelf #6	1	1x10 pine	5⅜ inches long

Tools

Measuring tape

Circular saw or miter saw

Cordless drill with drivers and bits

Speed square or combination square

Framing square

4 bar clamps, at least 36 inches long

Rubber mallet

Random-orbit sander with pads from 80 to 220 grit

Eye and ear protection

Optional Tools

2 bar clamps, 6 feet long

Fasteners

104 square-drive finish screws, 2¼ inches long

Glue

Instructions

The main skill needed to build this project is patience. The cuts are easy and the assembly very basic. However, there are 25 interlocking components in this project connected with over 100 screws. Each piece needs to be cut to exactly the right length to make these butt joints go together tight and look good. The only difference between an elegant showpiece and a hobby project relegated to the garage is going to be your frame of mind while building. Unless otherwise specified, use three 2¼-inch finish screws to attach each joint.

1 Cut the top, base, and sides of the main box to length. Drill three clearance holes for the finish screws ⅜ inch in from each end of the top and base, then glue and clamp the main box together as configured in the plans. If you don't have 6-foot-long bar clamps, use a corner clamp to line up the bottom of each joint and drill pilot holes through all of your clearance holes. If you do have 6-foot bar clamps and are using very soft wood, like the white pine shown here, there is no need to drill pilot holes before screwing the box.

2 Cut all of the pieces for the three interior boxes. Label each lightly with a pencil and stack the pieces for each box together. Drill three clearance holes ⅜ inch from both ends of the tops and bases of interior boxes #2 and #3. Drill clearance holes through only one end of the top and base of interior box #1. Glue, clamp, and screw the three boxes together. Interior box #1 will have only three sides at this point. Fill all holes and sand these three boxes through at least 150 grit. Sand the interior surfaces of the main box as well. Sanding now prevents you from sanding inside tight corners once the project is assembled.

3 Lay the main box down, face-up, on your worktable or floor. Set the three interior boxes approximately in place inside the main box (see photo A). Cut and install dividers and shelves as shown in the plans. Start at the bottom of the project by attaching divider #1 to the base of the main box. Attach interior box #1 to the main box and then to divider #1. Continue installing shelves, dividers, and boxes in sequence, moving from bottom to top (see photo B).

Glue and clamp each part in place. If you are using white pine or similar softwood, you probably won't need to do any predrilling. If you don't predrill and start getting any splitting around the screw, go back to our trusty clearance hole and pilot hole

SETTING THE STAGE. **With the main box positioned securely on a work surface, set the interior boxes approximately in place. As you install shelves and dividers, this arrangement helps keep you oriented as you refer to the drawing and Parts List.**

combination. Since the actual dimensions of your project may vary slightly from ours, don't just cut components based solely on the measurements given in the Parts List. Measure as you go and adjust the dimensions to fit the real-world project taking form in front of you.

This fact of life will probably be most obvious when you get to the last piece, divider #4. That's why we didn't even bother including a length for that piece—it's certain to vary, at least a little, from our measurement. Measure the interior dimension between the top of the main box and the top of interior box #3, then cut divider #4 to that length.

Finally, unless you have a very small drill, you won't be able to get three screws into the shelves and dividers attached to interior box # 3. In this situation, two screws are sufficient—one near each edge of each piece. Even then, you may need to drill at an angle in order to attach the screws.

4 Fill imperfections with wood putty appropriate to your chosen finish and sand the project as described on page 28. Wipe all the sawdust off the project using a tack cloth, then finish the project as desired. The project pictured here was finished with several coats of a dark, espresso brown stain, followed by a coat of clear acrylic sealer.

Notes on Installation

In order to prevent this project from tipping over and the obvious danger this event could entail, the bookcase should be securely attached to a solid surface such as a wall, floor, or ceiling. For example, at our house, I attached this project to a wall with an angle bracket screwed to the top of the main box and a wall stud. The possible options for connections are too numerous to outline here. If you aren't confident that your plan for installation is safe, ask someone with experience to help you.

FROM BOTTOM TO TOP. **Starting at the bottom of the main box, glue, clamp, and screw each component in place as illustrated in the plans.**

Storage Suite

The next three projects in the book—Shelves with Swivel Table, Chest of Drawers, and Cabinet with Glass Doors—are designed to stand alone or be combined as a single piece of furniture. One goal of this design is to illustrate that a large, seemingly complicated piece becomes much less intimidating if you break it up into sections, or, in the vernacular of this book, into separate boxes.

The first installment takes the basic run-of-the-mill shelving unit and adds a retractable table under the second shelf. Once you've built this design, you may find yourself adding these retractable tables to other pieces of furniture around the house.

Then we walk you through the chest of drawers. Last, you'll make the cabinet with glass doors. The best part is, they can work together or separately.

Shelves with Swivel Table

Tools

Measuring tape

Circular saw or miter saw

Cordless drill with drivers and bits

Speed square or combination square

Framing square

2 bar clamps, at least 36 inches long

Rubber mallet

Jigsaw

Random-orbit sander with discs from 60 to 220 grit

Eye and ear protection

Optional Tools

Countersink bit

2 bar clamps, 6 feet long

Fasteners

30 square-drive finish screws, 2¼ inches long

2 square-drive finish screws, 1⅝ inches long

Glue

Parts List

Part	Qty.	Material	Dimensions
Top	1	1x10 pine	29 inches long
Base	1	1x10 pine	29 inches long
Sides	2	1x10 pine	62½ inches long
Shelves	3	1x10 pine	27½ inches long
Swivel table	1	1x10 pine	26½ inches long
Lazy Susan hardware	1		6 x 6 inches
Table rest	1	1x2 pine scrap	3 inches long

Shelves with Swivel Table Plans

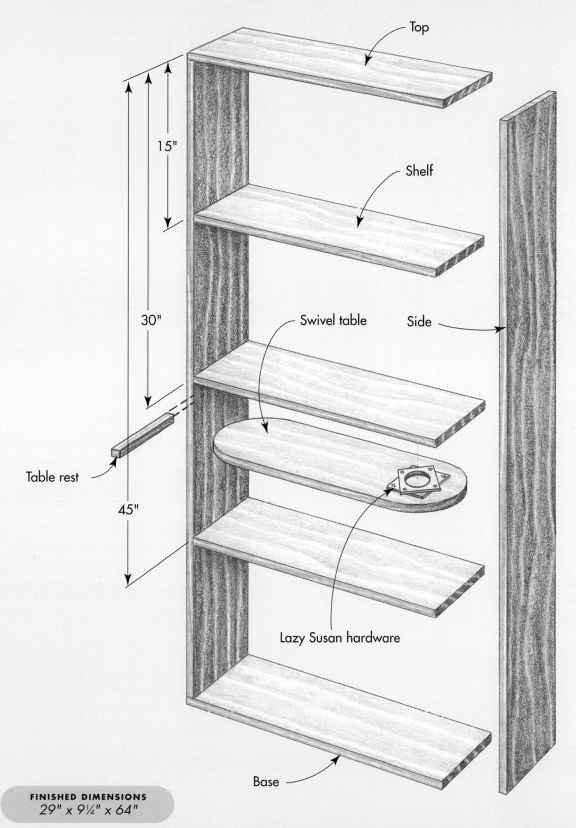

Top

Shelf

15"

30"

Swivel table

Side

Table rest

45"

Lazy Susan hardware

Base

FINISHED DIMENSIONS
29" x 9¼" x 64"

Notes on Materials

I selected southern yellow pine for this project because it has a nice grain for the pickled finish we chose. It's also a strong wood that provides good support for the swivel table.

Lazy Susan swivel-bearing hardware comes in many shapes and sizes. The easiest type to install is round with a hole in the middle, like a record. (For you youngsters, that's round like a CD with a hole in the middle.) This style requires only one screw and no fastidious measuring. In my experience, the more commonly available hardware consists of bearings sandwiched between two rectangular metal plates (see the plans on page 85). This hardware is a little more difficult to install. I decided to use it in this project because it may be the only style you can find.

Instructions

Unless otherwise specified, use three 2¼-inch finish screws to attach each joint.

1 Cut the top, base, and sides of the box to size. Drill three clearance holes for the finish screws ⅜ inch from each end of the top and base. Glue, clamp, and screw the box together as configured in the plans. If you don't have 6-foot-long bar clamps, use a corner clamp to line up the bottom of each joint and drill pilot holes through all of the clearance holes before screwing.

2 Cut the shelves and install them as illustrated in the drawing. However, we're far enough into this book for you to loosen up a bit. We chose to install only three shelves spaced widely apart, but there's no reason you couldn't add more shelves to fit your particular needs. The only thing to remember is that one shelf needs to hold the swivel table—be sure to place this shelf about ½ inch above your desired table height. Drill three clearance holes for each joint between the case and the shelf.

(Since our puttied screw holes will show through our chosen finish, we used a countersink bit that will leave a nice symmetrical hole after the screws are in place.) Glue and clamp the shelves in place. Drill pilot holes through the clearance holes and screw the shelves into place.

3 Cut the swivel table to length. Using the bottom of a five-gallon bucket, large can, or other cylindrical object at least 9¼ inches in diameter, draw an arc at each end of your table, as shown in photos A and B. Now, clamp the swivel table to your work surface and carefully cut out the shape of the arc with a jigsaw. Use 60-grit sandpaper on a random-orbit sander to fine-tune the shape of the arc, and repeat the process at the other end of the board. If you like, you can use your sander to soften the sharp edge on the top and bottom of the arc on the end of the table—this arc will be visible when

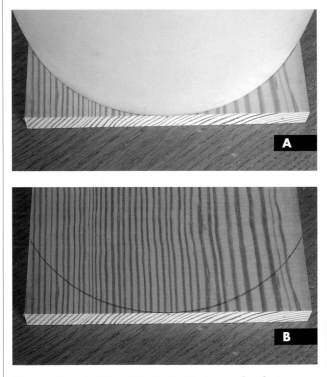

ROUND THE ENDS OF THE TABLE. **Use a bucket, can, or similar object with at least a 9¼-inch diameter to draw an arc on each end of the swivel table, then use a jigsaw to cut out the arcs.**

the table swings out. The basic arc shaping isn't only for looks. You need to take off the corners of the table so that it will be able to swing freely. If you don't have a jigsaw, cut a triangle off each corner of the table. The two triangles at each end should start about an inch down the side from the corner and meet each other at the middle of the end of the board. You're basically taking off the same wood as with the arc, but without the fancy shaping.

4 Fill all holes and imperfections with wood putty that matches your chosen finish. Sand all surfaces of the shelving unit and the swivel table as described on page 28. Sanding now will protect the bearings of the lazy Susan hardware from the fine sawdust produced while sanding.

5 Install your chosen lazy Susan hardware so that the side of the swivel table lines up with the side of the shelf above it. To allow for easy movement of the table, there should be about ¼ inch between each end of the table and the shelf unit. For details specific to your particular hardware's installation, refer to the instructions that came with it, and see the Notes on Materials for my recommendations.

6 Fill screw holes with an appropriate wood putty and sand them with 220-grit paper. Wipe off all sawdust using a tack cloth and finish the project as desired. The project pictured here was finished with several coats of a white wash pickling stain, followed by a coat of clear acrylic sealer.

Notes on Installation and Usage

This project was designed to be attached to the chest of drawers (see page 88) as part of the three-piece combo described at the beginning of these instructions. If you are building all three pieces, simply attach this project to the chest of drawers with four 1¼-inch wood screws—two near the front of the bookshelf and two near the back. If you intend for this project to stand alone, it should be attached to a wall to prevent it from tipping over. There are many options for doing this, and the right solution will depend on the type of wall and particular situation you are up against. See page 32 for basic guidelines on wall mounting, or ask someone in the hardware section at your building supply to recommend the best hardware for your situation.

The swivel table on this unit is light duty. It will easily hold a plate with food, a drink, and the book you're reading. It isn't, however, designed for heavier tasks such as ironing clothes or doing chin-ups. I spaced the shelves wide apart on this project with the idea that they would hold blankets and piles of sweaters as well as books. If you were to fill a shelf completely with large, oversized books, it is possible that the shelf would sag a bit or the project would lean to one side or the other. If that's a concern, you can add a back to the project. Refer to the bathroom cabinet (page 117) or the wardrobe (page 136) projects for instructions on adding a back.

Chest of Drawers

In the second component of our three-piece ensemble, the basic box is symmetrically divided into ten identical compartments and each is filled with a drawer.

I've simplified construction by avoiding dadoed joints for our shelves, a task that would take real precision in this context. Instead, you'll learn to insert fasteners at an angle, a simple, handy skill called *toenailing*. Though some chests of drawers are huge, cavernous vaults, this one has a thinner profile, allowing it to fit into a lot of places that its larger cousins can't. This chest also has a lot of smaller drawers, which give you many organizational options.

Chest of Drawers Plans

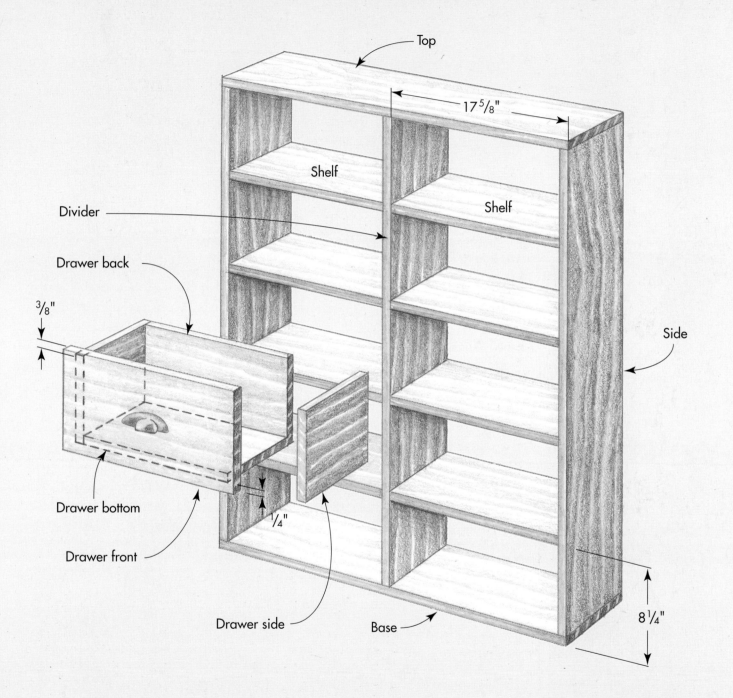

Top

17⁵⁄₈"

Shelf

Divider

Shelf

Drawer back

³⁄₈"

Side

Drawer bottom

Drawer front

¹⁄₄"

Drawer side

Base

8¹⁄₄"

FINISHED DIMENSIONS
36" x 10" x 42"

Parts List

Part	Qty.	Material	Dimensions
Top	1	1x10 pine	36 inches long
Base	1	1x10 pine	36 inches long
Sides	2	1x10 pine	40 ½ inches long
Divider	1	1x10 pine	40 ½ inches long
Shelves	8	1x10 pine	16 ⅞ inches long
Drawer sides	20	1x8 pine	9 inches long
Drawer back	10	1x8 pine	15 ⅛ inches long
Drawer bottom	10	1x10 pine	ripped to 8 ¼ inches wide x 15 ⅛ inches long
Drawer front	10	1x10 pine	ripped to 7 ⅞ inches wide x 17 ⅜ inches long
Drawer pulls	10	Any style	

Tools

Measuring tape

Circular saw or miter saw

Cordless drill with drivers and bits

Speed square or combination square

2 bar clamps, at least 48 inches long

Rubber mallet

Random-orbit sander with pads from 60 to 220 grit

Eye and ear protection

Optional Tools

Table saw

Fasteners

180 finish screws, 1 ⅝ inches long

Glue

Instructions

This project is straightforward, but it calls for a lot of precision. There are many identical parts that need to be cut and then assembled into identical components. The visual impact of the piece rests on the clean lines created by the symmetrical layout of the drawer fronts. This in turn depends on the symmetry of the drawer construction and placement of the shelves. In other words, every step is very simple, but needs to be executed accurately. If you pay attention and make your cuts and joints carefully, it will be a breeze. All joints are connected with 1⅝-inch finish screws. Unless specified otherwise, use three screws per joint.

1 Cut the top, base, sides, and divider of the box to length. Drill three clearance holes for your finish screws ⅜ inch from each end of the top and base. Also drill three clearance holes 18 inches from either end (i.e., through the exact center of the top and base). Glue, clamp, and screw the box together as configured in the plans.

2 Cut the shelves to length, then mark their placement on the inside faces of the sides and both faces of the divider. The shelves need to be spaced evenly inside the box. The bottom of each shelf should be 8¼ inches from the bottom of the shelf above and below it, as illustrated in the plans. Install all four shelves on the right side of the project by drilling clearance holes, gluing, clamping, and screwing (see photo A).

INSTALLING THE SHELVES. **Install all four shelves on the right side of the box first.**

3 To install the shelves on the left side, start at the top and drill two clearance holes through the divider at each shelf location. Drill these holes at an angle so that the screw will enter the shelf. This sort of angled fastening is called *toenailing*. Next, drill

clearance holes for the shelves through the left side of the box. Glue and clamp a shelf in place. Attach the shelf to the side of the box first, then to the divider. Toenailing has a tendency to push the board away from the fastener, thus moving the joint out of alignment. To prevent the shelf from moving as you drive the screw home, cut a 7½-inch-long spacer and set it in place under the shelf you are toenailing. Predrill through the toenailed clearance holes into the shelf, then screw the shelf in place against the divider (see photo B). Repeat this same process for the other three shelves.

TOENAILING. **Using a spacer to help keep things aligned, clamp a shelf in place. Predrill through the toenailed clearance hole and drive a screw through the divider into the shelf.**

Chest of Drawers

4 Cut all drawer sides, bottoms, fronts, and backs to length. After drilling clearance holes, glue, clamp, and screw these pieces together, as shown in the plans. Screw the sides to the backs first, then attach the bottoms.

5 Lay a drawer front on your worktable so that the front face is against the work surface. Draw a line along the length of the board ¼ inch from one edge and another through the width of the board ⅜ inch in from each end. Drill clearance holes ⅜ inch inside each of these lines—three holes on each side and two along the bottom (see photo C). Glue and clamp the drawer in place so the outside edges of the bottom and sides rest on these lines, then screw the front to the drawer (see photo D). Repeat this step until all 10 drawers are assembled.

D

ATTACHING THE DRAWER FRONTS. **Glue and clamp the drawer flush with the pencil lines on the drawer front and screw it in place. The drawer front should overhang the top of the drawer box by ⅜ inch and the bottom by ¼ inch.**

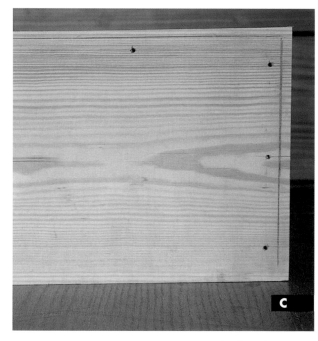

C

PREPPING THE DRAWER FRONTS. **Mark the placement of the drawer on the back of each drawer front and then drill clearance holes ⅜ inch inside these lines.**

6 Fill any holes and imperfections with wood putty appropriate to your chosen finish, then sand the project as described on page 28. The interior of the box and the bottom of the drawers only need to be sanded through 100 grit—just enough to knock down rough spots that might prevent the drawer from sliding smoothly. Wipe away any sawdust using a tack cloth and then finish the project as desired. The project pictured here was finished with several coats of a whitewash pickling stain, followed by a coat of clear acrylic sealer.

7 Attach the drawer pulls of your choice.

Cabinet with Glass Doors

The final installment of this three-piece set starts with a smaller version of the box used on the chest of drawers.

Because I've added a back and simple doors, this project serves well as a beginner's introduction to door construction. To spruce up the doors a bit, I added glass and applied mullions to simulate multiple panes of glass. The resulting cabinet can be used as a bookshelf, a display case, or to store clothes.

Cabinet with Glass Doors Plans

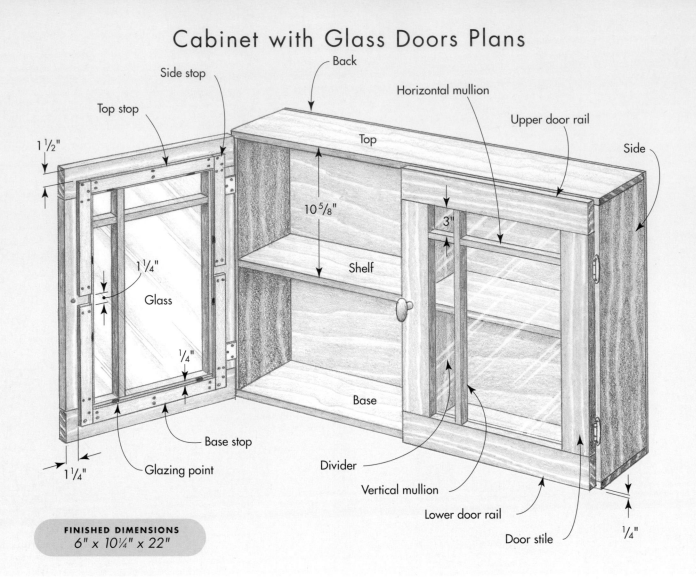

Back

Top stop

Side stop

Horizontal mullion

Upper door rail

Side

1½"

Top

10⅝"

3"

Shelf

1¼"

Glass

¼"

Base

Base stop

Divider

Vertical mullion

1¼"

Glazing point

Lower door rail

Door stile

¼"

FINISHED DIMENSIONS
6" x 10¼" x 22"

Tools

Measuring tape

Circular saw or miter saw

Cordless drill with drivers and bits

Speed square or combination square

4 bar clamps, at least 24 inches long

Rubber mallet

Random-orbit sander with pads from 60 to 220 grit

Putty knife

Eye and ear protection

Optional Tools

Table saw

Fasteners

30 finish screws, 1⅜ inches long

20 finish nails, 1 inch long

72 #8 wood screws, 1¼ inches long

16 glazing points

Glue

Parts List

Part	Qty.	Material	Dimensions
Top	1	1x10 pine	36 inches long
Base	1	1x10 pine	36 inches long
Sides	2	1x10 pine	20½ inches long
Divider	1	1x10 pine	20½ inches long
Shelves	2	1x10 pine	ripped to 9 inches wide x 16⅞ inches long
Back	1	¼ inch lauan plywood	36 inches long x 22 inches wide
Upper door rails	2	1x4 pine	17¼ inches long
Lower door rails	2	1x4 pine	17¼ inches long
Door stiles	4	1x4 pine	ripped to 3¼ inches wide x 14½ inches long
Top stop	2	1x4 pine	ripped to 1¾ inches wide x 11¼ inches long
Base stop	2	1x4 pine	ripped to 1¾ inches wide x 11¼ inches long
Side stops	8	1x4 pine	ripped to 1¾ inches wide x 8⅜ inches long
Glass	2	1⁄16-inch-thick clear glass	11⅛ x 14⅞ inches
Hinges	2	adjustable overlay, face frame mount	see Notes on Materials
Vertical mullion	2	1x pine	ripped to ¾ inches wide x 14½ inches long
Long horizontal mullion	2	1x pine	ripped to ¾ inches wide x 7 inches long
Short horizontal mullion	2	1x pine	ripped to ¾ inches wide x 3 inches long
Door handle	1	Any style	
Door catches	2	Any style	

Notes on Materials

The door dimensions listed in the Parts List are based on using a hinge that mounts to the edge (thickness) of the sides of the cabinet and hold the side of the doors ½ inch in from the side of the cabinet. There are several types of hinges that can accomplish this. The creature I recommend is called a *variable overlay, face frame mount hinge*. The section of this hinge that connects to the box needs to be no more than ½ inch wide. The hinge plate that attaches to the door needs to be no more than 1½ inches wide.

Instructions

Your focus in this project should be on the doors. Double doors hanging side by side have to be built and hung very accurately. In order for a simple design like this to work, the tops and bottoms of both doors must line up with each other, while also creating an even gap between the two doors where they meet.

1 Cut the top, base, sides, and divider of the box to size. Drill three clearance holes for the finish screws ⅜ inch from each end of the top and base. Also drill three clearance holes 18 inches from either end (i.e., through the exact centers) of the top and base to accommodate the divider. Glue, clamp, and screw the box together with finish screws.

2 Rip and cut the shelves to length. Drill three clearance holes for finish screws through both sides of the box and the divider (11 inches down from the top of the box). Mark shelf placement, as seen in the plans, on the inside faces of the sides and both faces of the dividers. Glue, clamp, and screw the right shelf into place with finish screws so that the back of the shelf is flush with the back of the box. When installed, this should create a ¼-inch reveal between the front of the shelf and the front of the box (see photo A). Drill two toenailed clearance holes through the divider starting at the top of the installed shelf. Glue and clamp the left shelf in place using a 9⅞-inch-long spacer set under the side of the shelf next to the divider. Screw the shelf to the side of the box with finish screws. At the divider, drill pilot holes through the toenailed clearance holes and then attach the shelf with finish screws.

3 Cut the back to size. Then lay the box face down and install the back with glue and 1-inch-long finish nails spaced 6 inches apart.

4 Cut all door and stop pieces to size. The stops can be made by first ripping 1x4 pine in half. After they're cut to size, drill clearance holes in the stops as shown in the plans. Apply glue to the thickness of the door rails and stiles where they will intersect, then clamp one door together face down on your worktable—using one clamp on each side should be plenty. With the door still clamped together, apply glue and install the stops by first drilling pilot holes through the clearance holes, then screwing the stops in place using 1¼-inch-long wood screws (see photo B). There should be a 1½-inch reveal between the top and base stops and the outer edge of the door and a 1¼-inch reveal between side stops and

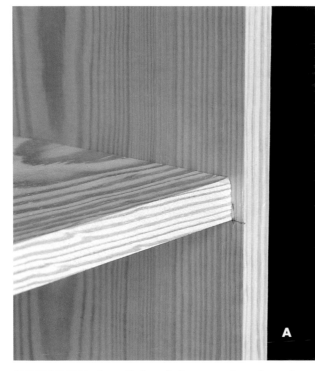

SHELF REVEAL. **Install the shelves so that there is a ¼-inch reveal between the shelf and the front of the box. This allows space for the glass that will be installed in the door.**

DOOR ASSEMBLY. **Glue and clamp the door together, then attach the stops. The purpose of these stops is to provide a surface to attach glazing points, but also they hold the door together and prevent warping.**

the outer edge. There should also be ¼-inch reveals between the stops and the interior edges of the door on all sides. The 1¼-inch gaps between the side stops make room for the shelf when the door is closed (see photo C). Repeat this entire process for the second door.

SPACING THE STOPS. **The gap between the side door stops allows the doors to close without hitting the shelves.**

5 Carefully cut the mullions and test their fit on the doors (as illustrated in the plans). It is important that they fit tightly because they're installed using only a bit of glue.

6 Fill any holes and imperfections with a wood putty appropriate to your chosen finish, then sand the project as described on page 28. Wipe off all sawdust with a tack cloth and finish all project components as desired. The project pictured here was finished with several coats of a whitewash pickling stain, followed by a coat of clear acrylic sealer.

7 Clean off your worktable and cover it with a soft cloth. Lay the doors face down on the table and set the glass in place between the stops. Using a putty knife, push glazing points into the stops to secure the glass. Use two points on the top and base stop and one on each side stop.

8 Turn the doors over. Apply a bit of glue to the endgrain of each mullion piece and push them carefully into place as configured in the plans. The top of the horizontal mullions should be set 3 inches from the bottom of the upper door rail.

9 Turn the doors over onto their faces again. Attach the hinges to the doors stiles so that the hinge plate is 1 inch away from the joint between the rails and stiles, as shown in the plans. Now, lay the box on the table and set the doors in place so that there is an even reveal created between the top and bottom of the doors and the box. There should also be an even ¼-inch gap between the doors. Drill pilot holes and screw the hinges to the box.

10 Install the handles and door catches of your choice. We chose a single round knob centered in the middle of the door stile and used simple magnetic closures, one attached next to the divider at the top of the case.

Notes on Installation

This shelf unit is designed to attach to the chest of drawers built in the previous chapter. A few thin, 1¼-inch wood screws through the base of this cabinet into the top of the chest of drawers are all that are needed to secure it in place. If you intend for this project to stand alone, it should be attached to whatever surface it sits on. Without such attachment, the empty unit may flip over when both doors are opened. Alternatively, you could simply screw the assembly to a wall. For more on wall mounting, see page 32 in the Basics chapter.

Coffee Table

For this next project you'll use the basic box in new ways. In designing it, I combined the front and rear table legs into two single open-sided boxes. The tabletop is supported by two of these leg assemblies, with one placed at each end.

This project also uses an internal shelf unit box to connect the long shelf to the tabletop, making both of them more rigid in the process. By using tile in the tabletop, this project also introduces mortar-less tile installation. All of this comes together to create a contemporary table with a Japanese look, as well as integrated book and magazine storage.

Coffee Table Plans

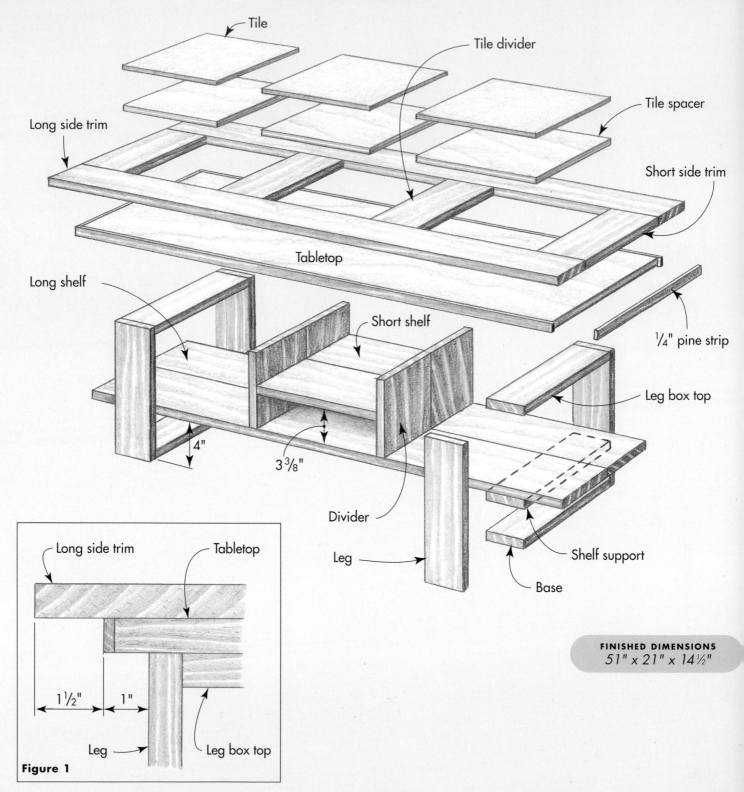

Tile

Tile divider

Tile spacer

Long side trim

Short side trim

Long shelf

Short shelf

Tabletop

4"

3 3/8"

Divider

Leg

Leg box top

$\frac{1}{4}$" pine strip

Shelf support

Base

FINISHED DIMENSIONS
51" x 21" x 14½"

Long side trim

Tabletop

1½"   1"

Leg

Leg box top

Figure 1

Parts List

Part	Qty.	Material	Dimensions
Leg	4	1x4 pine	13 inches long
Base	2	1x4 pine	14½ inches long
Leg box top	2	1x4 pine	14½ inches long
Shelf support	2	1x4 pine	14½ inches long
Tabletop	1	¾-inch plywood capped with ¼-inch pine strips	18 x 48 inches
Long shelf	2	1x8 pine	48 inches long
Dividers	4	1x8 pine	7½ inches long
Short shelf	2	1x8 pine	12 inches long
Long side trim	2	1x6 pine	ripped to 4⅜ inches wide x 51 inches long
Short side trim	2	1x4 pine	ripped to 4⅜ x 11¾ inches long
Tile dividers	2	1x4 pine	ripped to 3¼ inches wide x 11¾ inches long
Tile spacers	3	½-inch plywood	11½ x 11½ inches
Tile	3	12 x 12 tile	11¾ x 11¾ x ¼ inches

Tools

Measuring tape

Circular saw or miter saw

Cordless drill with drivers and bits

Speed square or combination square

Framing square

2 bar clamps, at least 36 inches long

Rubber mallet

Random-orbit sander with pads from 60 to 220 grit

Eye and ear protection

Optional Tools

Table saw

Fasteners

60 finish screws, 1⅝ inches long

30 #6 wood screws, 1¼ inches long

20 brad nails, 1 inch long

45 finish nails, 1¼ inch long

30 #6 wood screws, 1 inch long

Glue

Instructions

1 Cut all the parts of the leg boxes to length. Drill two clearance holes for finish screws ⅜ inch in from both ends of each leg. Glue and clamp the leg boxes together as configured in the plans, then screw them together.

2 Cut the shelf supports to size. Drill two clearance holes for finish screws 4⅜ inches up from the bottom of each leg. Glue, clamp, and attach the shelf supports with finish screws.

3 Cut the long shelves to length. Set the leg boxes on your work table or the floor. Apply glue and clamp the long shelves in place so that they overhang the shelf supports by 4 inches (see photo A). Drill pilot holes for 1¼-inch wood screws through the shelves into the support. Each end of each shelf should have two holes near the outer edge of the support and two holes near the edge of the support. Once the pilot holes are drilled, screw the shelves in place.

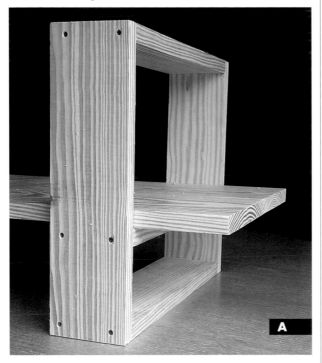

ATTACHING THE LONG SHELF. **The shelf should overhang the leg assembly by 4 inches on both ends.**

4 To make the tabletop, cut a 17½ inch x 47½-inch piece of ¾-inch CDX plywood. You'll then use thin strips of pine to cover the raw edges of the plywood. To do this, rip three ¼-inch-wide pieces from a 4-foot-long 1x4. From these rips, cut four pieces: two 17½ inches long and two 48 inches long. Apply glue and attach the 17½-inch pieces to the width of the plywood using 1-inch-long brad nails spaced every 8 inches. Then apply the two 48-inch pieces in the same fashion. When finished, the raw edges of the plywood should be covered on all four sides (see photo B).

BOXING OUT THE PLYWOOD TABLETOP. **To cover the end grain on the plywood top, glue and nail ¼-inch pine strips to all four sides.**

5 Glue and clamp the tabletop to the leg assemblies. The tabletop should over hang the leg assemblies by 4 inches at each end (just like the long shelf) and by 1 inch at the front and back, as shown in figure 1. Attach the tabletop to the leg box tops using three pairs of 1¼-inch wood screws. As long as you make sure that the screws enter the leg box top at least 1 inch away from the joint with the legs, there is no need to predrill.

6 Cut the short shelves and the dividers to size. Drill clearance holes, glue, and clamp both shelves between two dividers as shown in the plans. Position one of these shelf assemblies so that it is centered on the long shelf and tabletop. (This means that the outside of each side of the units will rest 17⅜ inches from each end of the long shelf and top.) Using two 1⅝-inch finish screws for each joint, attach the shelf assembly to the tabletop and long shelf. Apply glue to the back of the shelf assembly, then clamp the second small shelf assembly to the first. Attach the second assembly in the same manner as you did the first.

7 Cut all trim pieces to size. Referring to the plans, apply glue and clamp the trim in place so that it overhangs the tabletop by 1½ inches, or evenly, on all sides. Attach the trim to the tabletop with pairs of 1¼-inch-long finish nails. Use five pairs on the long sides and three pairs on the short sides.

Note: The trim and divider measurements provided here are based on tile 11¾ x 11¾ inches. In my experience, tile dimensions can vary from style to style and sometimes even batch to batch. Measure your actual tile and adjust the trim if needed.

8 Cut the tile dividers. Apply glue and install the dividers, evenly spaced, between the side trim so that three 11¾-inch-square boxes are formed on the top of the table as shown in the plans. Attach each divider with two pairs of 1¼-inch-long finish nails.

Note: the following instructions are based on plywood spacers that are actually ½ thick and tile that is actually ¼ inch thick. If your materials don't match these measurements, you'll need to make adjustments. For example, some nominal ½-inch plywood has an actual thickness of ⁷⁄₁₆ inch. If this is the case, set ¹⁄₁₆-inch-thick wood or cardboard shims under the spacers before installing them.

PREPARING FOR TILE. **Glue and screw the tile spacers inside the trimmed-out boxes on top of the table. Drill 1-inch holes through each box to make it easier to remove tiles should you ever need to.**

9 Cut the tile spacers to fit inside the three boxes on the top of the table. Apply glue and install the spacers using 1-inch wood screws inside. Then use a 1-inch spade bit to drill holes through the spacers and the tabletop (see photo C).

10 Fill any holes and imperfections with a wood putty appropriate to your chosen finish, then sand the project as described on page 28. Wipe off all sawdust with a tack cloth and finish all of the project components as desired. The sample project here was first covered with a coat of primer tinted gray and then finished with several coats of black gloss latex enamel paint. The project was sanded with 220-grit paper between each coat.

11 Set the tile into place on top of the spacers. I recommend placing the tile without adhesive. That way, if a tile breaks or you want to change the tile color someday, you can just pop them out by using the holes you drilled through the tile spacers and the tabletop.

Wine Rack

This project is basically a big box filled with 24 smaller boxes. To build it, you won't need to learn any new woodworking skills, but your ability for precision will be tested. The compartments are designed for both standard three-quarter and one-and-a-half liter bottles. However, wine isn't the only thing you can store in this project. We use one near the front door as a place to hold things like gloves, small tools such as pruning shears, mail waiting to be posted, and...well, you know how it goes—storage fills up quickly when it's conveniently located.

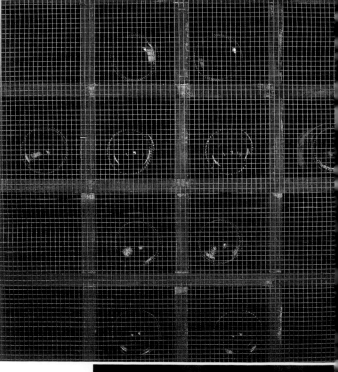

Wine Rack Plans

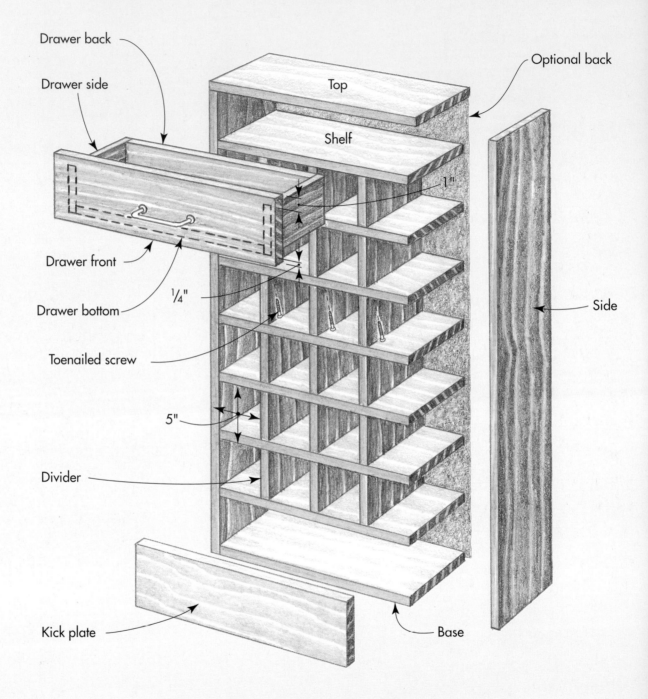

Drawer back

Drawer side

Top

Shelf

Optional back

1"

Drawer front

¼"

Drawer bottom

Side

Toenailed screw

5"

Divider

Kick plate

Base

FINISHED DIMENSIONS
20¾" x 10" x 40¾"

Parts List

Part	Qty.	Material	Dimensions
Top	1	1x10 pine	20¾ inches long
Base	1	1x10 pine	19¼ inches long
Sides	2	1x10 pine	40 inches long
Shelves	7	1x10 pine	19¼ inches long
Dividers	18	1x10 pine	4¼ inches long
Drawer sides	2	1x6 pine	ripped to 4 inches wide x 9 inches long
Drawer back	1	1x6 pine	ripped to 4 inches wide x 17⅝ inches long
Drawer bottom	1	1x10 pine	ripped to 8¼ inches wide x 17⅝ inches long
Drawer front	1	1x6 pine	ripped to 5¼ inches wide x 20¾ long
Kick plate	1	1x6 pine	ripped to 5¼ inches wide x 20¾ long
Back	1	hardware cloth or burlap	40½ inches long x 20½ inches wide
Drawer pull	1	Any style	

Tools

- Measuring tape
- Circular saw or miter saw
- Cordless drill with drivers and bits
- Speed square or combination square
- 2 bar clamps, at least 48 inches long
- Rubber mallet
- Random-orbit sander with pads from 60 to 220 grit
- Eye and ear protection

Optional Tools

- Table saw

Fasteners

- 175 finish screws, 1⅝ inches long
- 25 roofing nails, ¾ inch long
- Glue

Notes on Materials

Though it isn't strictly necessary, I chose to install a back on this project so that the bottles would all protrude the same distance from the front of the rack. I used a heavy metal mesh called *hardware cloth* for this purpose, but burlap or muslin would also work.

Instructions

This project is mostly about focusing on what you're doing and not getting sloppy. Because you're creating the same joint over and over again in a symmetrical matrix, use your spacer for every joint, and clamp it securely before screwing it in. If you follow that advice, this project will go quickly and come out beautifully. All joints are connected with 1⅝-inch finish screws. Use three screws per joint, unless otherwise noted.

1 Cut the sides, shelves, and dividers to size, as well as an extra divider to use as a spacer (see photo A). Sand both faces of the dividers and shelves and one face of each side piece with 100- and 150-grit paper.

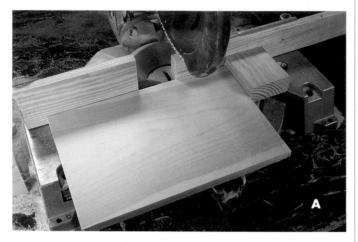

MAKING REPEATED CUTS. **To cut the dividers, I used this simple jig attached to my miter saw. The block at right acts as a stop, ensuring that each piece is cut to exactly the same length.**

2 Mark the shelf locations on the sanded faces of the sides. The shelves are evenly spaced 5 inches apart, as shown in the plans. Clamp the box sides together on your worktable and drill three clearance holes for each shelf and for the base (see photo B).

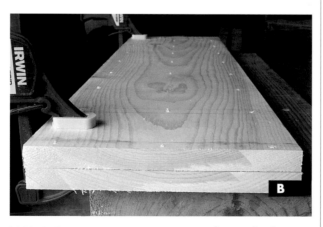

PREPPING THE SIDES FOR SHELVES. **Clamp the box sides, marked face side up, to your worktable and drill clearance holes for the shelving. Also drill three clearance holes ⅜ inch from one end of the sides to secure the base.**

3 Mark both faces of each shelf for the dividers as shown in the plans. Clamp the shelves together two at a time, then drill clearance holes for the dividers.

4 Glue, clamp, and screw the lowest shelf into place between the sides, then glue, clamp, and screw the dividers onto the shelf from underneath. Glue, clamp, and screw the second shelf to the box sides and then to the dividers below it.

5 The third shelf is installed in the same way, but the dividers are then pushed into place between the second and third shelf. Use the extra divider you cut as a spacer between the divider and the side of the box. Then clamp the two shelves to the divider and screw the third shelf into the divider. Toenail a pilot hole through the second shelf into the divider, then sink a screw through the pilot hole and into the divider. Move the spacer over and repeat this process for the other two dividers. Then turn the project over and toenail screws to secure the back of the dividers, just as you did the fronts. Don't forget to use the

ATTACHING DIVIDERS. **Using a spacer to keep things uniform, glue and clamp each divider into place. Attach the divider to the upper shelf first, then toenail through the lower shelf into the divider.**

spacer and clamp on the back. Continue this process until all of the shelves and dividers are installed (see photo C).

6 Cut the top and base to size. Drill clearance holes ⅜ inch from each end of the top piece. Glue, clamp, and screw these pieces to the sides as configured in the plans. Notice that the sides sandwich the base and are capped by the top.

7 Cut the drawer pieces to size. Predrill, glue, clamp, and screw the drawer sides, back, and bottom together as configured in the plans. Attach the drawer front so that it overhangs ¹³/₁₆ inch beyond each side of the drawer (see photo D).

8 Cut the kick plate to size then glue and clamp the kick plate to the base of the box. The ends and bottom of the kick plate should be flush with the sides and base of the box. The top of the kick plate should create a ½-inch reveal with the first shelf. Drill two pilot holes through the kick plate near each end and three pilot holes along the bottom. Attach the ends and bottom to the sides and base of the box with screws.

9 Fill any holes and imperfections with wood putty appropriate to your chosen finish, then sand the project as described on page 28. Wipe off all sawdust with a tack cloth and finish the project as desired. The sample project pictured was first covered with a coat of primer, then finished with several coats of latex flat enamel paint and a final coat of a satin clear coat sealer. The project was sanded with 220-grit paper between each coat.

10 After the finish has dried, cut the back and attach it to the back of the wine rack so that it covers all the cubbyholes. Use roofing nails spaced every 8 inches to secure the back.

11 Install your chosen drawer pull.

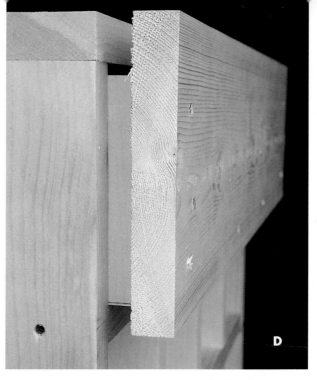

PLACING THE DRAWER FRONT. **Attach the drawer front so that it overhangs the sides of the drawer by ¹³/₁₆ inch. This will make the front flush with the sides of the box when closed and give a ¹/₁₆-inch clearance between the drawer and each box side to allow the drawer to open and close.**

Storage Chest

In this project, rather than using plywood or another sheet material, you'll manufacture your own wide components using off-the-shelf lumber, and then you'll use these pieces to build one big box that is divided into several smaller boxes. Once you're comfortable with the technique, you can use regular lumber to replace sheet materials in many furniture applications. Here, it gives the finished chest a traditional look. The chest has two big drawers and three compartments accessible by lifting the lid. It makes a great storage chest, but I designed it wide enough to serve as a window seat, as well.

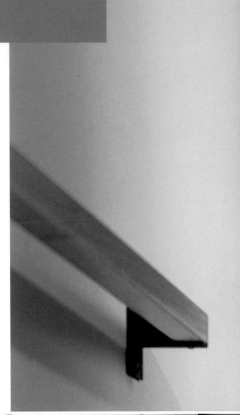

Storage Chest Plans

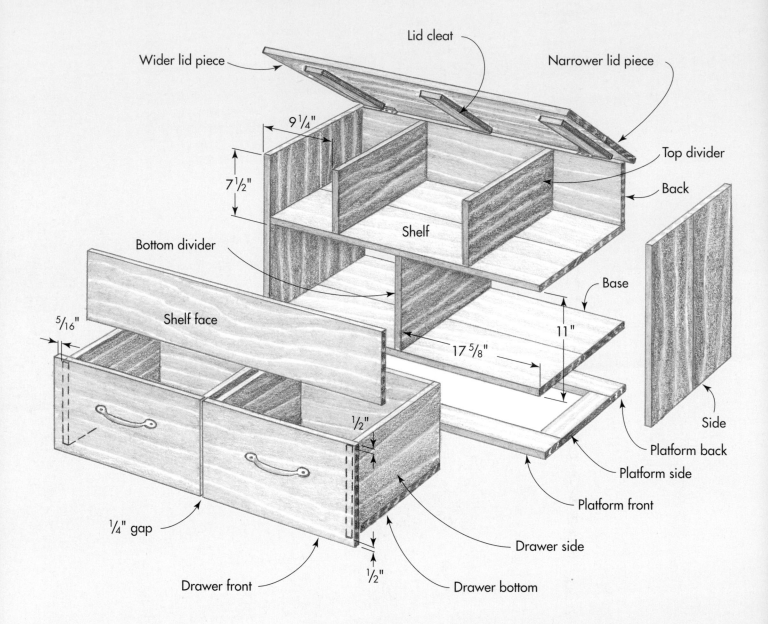

Wider lid piece

Lid cleat

Narrower lid piece

Top divider

Back

9¼"

7½"

Bottom divider

Shelf

Shelf face

Base

11"

17⅝"

Side

⁵⁄₁₆"

½"

Platform back

Platform side

Platform front

¼" gap

Drawer side

½"

Drawer front

½"

Drawer bottom

FINISHED DIMENSIONS
37" x 19¼" x 20"

Parts List

Part	Qty.	Material	Dimensions
Sides	4	1 x 10 pine	18½ inches long
Base	2	1 x 10 pine	34½ inches long
Shelf	2	1 x 10 pine	34½ inches long
Bottom divider	1	1 x 12 pine	ripped to 10¼ inches wide and 18½ inches long
Top dividers	2	1 x 8 pine	ripped to 6¾ inches wide x 17¾ inches long
Back	1	1 x 8 pine	ripped to 6¾ x 34½ inches long
Platform front	1	1 x 4 pine	35½ inches long
Platform back	1	1 x 4 pine	35½ inches long
Platform sides	2	1 x 4 pine	11 inches long
Drawer sides	4	1 x 10 pine	18 inches long
Drawer backs	2	1 x 10 pine	15¼ inches long
Drawer bottoms	2	¾ plywood	18 x 16¾ inches
Drawer fronts	2	1 x 12 pine	ripped to 11 inches wide x 17⅜ inches long
Shelf face	1	1 x 8 pine	ripped to 7 inches wide x 35½ inches long
Narrower lid piece	1	1 x 10 pine	37 inches long
Wider lid piece	1	1 x 12 pine	ripped to 10¼ inches wide x 37 inches long
Lid cleats	3	1 x 4 pine	16 inches long
Hinges	2	½-inch overlay, partial wrap hinge	see Notes on Materials
Top holder	1	light gauge chain	19 inches long
Drawer pulls	2	Any style	

Tools

Measuring tape

Circular saw or miter saw

Cordless drill with drivers and bits

Speed square or combination square

4 bar clamps, at least 36 inches long

Rubber mallet

Random-orbit sander with pads from 60 to 220 grit

Eye and ear protection

Optional Tools

Table saw

Fasteners

100 finish screws, 1⅝ inches long

24 wood screws, 1¼ inches long

Glue

Notes on Materials

The hinges I used for this project sound complicated: ½-inch overlay partial wrap hinge. In fact, they are among the easiest hinges to install because they don't require mortising. One side attaches to the inside face of the back of the box and the other attaches to the inside face of the lid. Choose hinges that are at least 2½ inches long with a leaf at least 2 inches wide.

Instructions

Your focus in this project is edge-gluing lumber to create wide components of solid wood. The secret here is to start with straight lumber, then carefully glue and clamp it together. Use as many clamps as it takes. If the boards just don't want to stay flush, you may want to dismantle the assembly, scrape off glue that has started to cure, and try again. On the other hand, small deviations can be removed easily with a random-orbit sander. Unless otherwise specified, joints are connected with three 1⅝-inch finish screws.

1 Cut the boards that make up the sides and base. Mark the shelf placement on the sides and drill clearance holes for the shelves and base pieces as shown in the plans.

2 Edge-glue the base pieces and two sets of side pieces. To do this, first apply glue to the thickness of each board where it will abut its partner, then set the pieces on your work table and clamp them together. Set a 2x4 or other scrap of wood across the width of each end of the laminated boards, then sandwich the edge-glued boards between the wood scrap and worktable with clamps. This will help keep the faces of the glued boards flush with one another. To prevent the glue that squeezes out at the joint from sticking to your wood scraps, cover them with waxed paper.

3 Glue, clamp, and screw the glued-up sides to the glued-up base, as shown in photo A.

4 Cut the shelf pieces to size and glue them together using the same method you used to join the sides and base. Cut the top dividers, then glue, clamp, and screw them to the shelf using the dimensions provided in the plans. The dividers should be flush with the front of the shelf, leaving a ¾-inch space at the back of the box to accommodate the back (see photo B). Glue, clamp, and screw the shelf unit to the sides of the box as shown in the drawing.

ASSEMBLING THE SHELF UNIT. **After edge-gluing the shelf, glue, clamp, and screw the top dividers in place. The front of the dividers are flush with the front of the shelf, leaving space at the back to attach the back piece.**

5 Cut the bottom divider. Glue, clamp, and screw it to the base and shelf as shown in the plans.

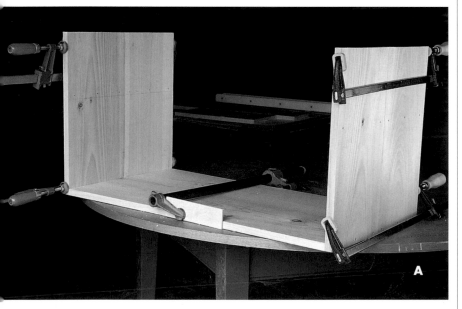

MAKE WIDE BOARDS FROM NARROW ONES. **Using glue and clamps, edge-glue the two base pieces together and two pairs of side pieces together. Then screw the sides to the base.**

6 Rip the back piece and cut it to length. Apply glue and clamp the back in place. Drill two pilot holes through each side of the box and two holes through the back into each divider. Then screw the back into place (see photo C).

INSTALLING THE BACK. **Set the back piece into the pocket created by the inset of the top dividers.**

7 Cut all four platform pieces to length. Apply glue and install them to the bottom of the base as shown in the plans. Use pairs of 1¼-inch wood screws spaced every 12 inches. The platform forms a box, creating a ¼-inch reveal on all sides with the base.

8 Cut the drawer pieces to size. Predrill, glue, clamp, and screw the drawer sides, back, and bottoms together as shown in the plans. Notice that the bottom caps the sides and that the back is inset atop the bottom and between the sides. Attach the drawer front as shown in the drawing. The drawer front should be centered so that it overhangs ⁵⁄₁₆ inch past each side of the drawer. This will allow the front of the installed drawer to overhang the side, shelf, and bottom divider by ¼ inch, while leaving ¹⁄₁₆ inch on each side of the drawer to allow it to slide open and closed.

9 Rip the shelf face and cut it to length. Install the shelf face to the shelf, top dividers, and sides of the front of the chest so that it is flush to the top edges of the sides and top dividers and overlaps the thickness of each side by ½ inch.

10 Cut the lid pieces and lid cleats. Edge-glue the top pieces together as you did for the shelves and other components in this project. With the lid still clamped together, apply glue and install the cleats so that their ends are 1¾ inches in from each side of the lid. The outer edge of the outside cleats should sit about 3 inches away from each end of the lid and the middle cleat should be centered. Screw the cleats in place using 1¼-inch wood screws (see photo D).

BUILDING THE LID. **Edge-glue the lid pieces together, then position the cleats so that they won't hit the box or the dividers as the lid closes.**

11 Attach the hinges to the inside face of the back of the box so that they are flush with the outside face of the top dividers (see photo E). Lay the box on its back and install the hinges to the lid. The lid should overhang the box ½ inch on each side. The overlay hinges create a ½-inch offset between the lid and the back of the box. In turn, the lid will overhang ½ inch past the front of the box.

12 Using ½-inch wood screws, attach one end of the chain to the left top cleat, about 5 inches down from its end. Attach the other end of the chain 7 inches in from the back of the box and 1½ inches down from the top of the box side.

ATTACHING THE LID. **Attach the hinges so that they are flush with the top dividers and allow the lid to overhang the sides by ½ inch. Installing the chain prevents the weight of the open lid from pulling against the hinges**

E

13 Fill any holes and imperfections with wood putty appropriate to your chosen finish and sand the project as described on page 28. Wipe off all sawdust with a tack cloth and finish the project as desired. The project pictured here was painted with several coats of eggshell latex paint. The project was sanded with 220-grit paper between each coat.

14 After the finish dries, install drawer pulls of your choice.

Bathroom Cabinet

One problem with store-bought storage furniture is that it often comes in only one size and style: big and clunky. This little cabinet breaks that mold—it has a thin profile and narrow width, allowing it to fit in some pretty tight places. Still, it's wide enough to store large towels, and look refined while doing so.

Included in this project are a few details that will add to your carpentry skills. For one thing, it features a fully concealed back set into rabbeted grooves. The legs are also fabricated from wooden dowels that are recessed into the base of the cabinet for added strength. The top of the cabinet is constructed using a modified mitered joint. In addition, the door glass is installed without the aid of stops.

Bathroom Cabinet Plans

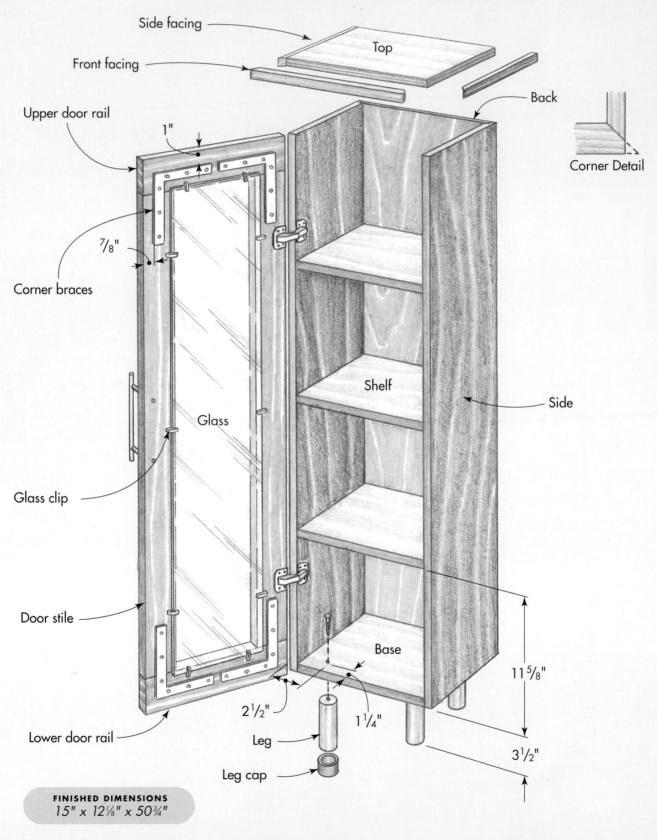

Side facing

Front facing

Top

Back

Corner Detail

Upper door rail

1"

7/8"

Corner braces

Glass

Shelf

Side

Glass clip

Door stile

Base

11⁵/₈"

Lower door rail

2¹/₂"

Leg

1¹/₄"

3¹/₂"

Leg cap

FINISHED DIMENSIONS
15" x 12¹/₈" x 50³/₄"

Parts List

Part	Qty.	Material	Dimensions
Top	1	1x12 pine	14 inches long
Front facing for top	1	1x pine	⅞ inches wide x 15¾ inches long
Side facing for top	2	1x pine	½ inches wide x 12½ inches long
Base	1	1x12	ripped to 11 inches wide x 12½ inches long
Sides	2	1x12 pine	46½ inches long
Back	1	¼-inch lauan	13⁷⁄₁₆ x 46½
Shelves	3	1x12 pine	ripped to 11 inches wide x 12½ inches long
Upper door rail	1	1x4 pine	ripped to 3 inches wide x 14 inches long
Lower door rail	1	1x4 pine	ripped to 3 inches wide x 14 inches long
Door stiles	2	1x4 pine	ripped to 3 inches wide x 40¼ inches long
Corner braces	4	90-degree angle brackets	arms 6 inches long x 1 inch wide
Legs	4	1⅛-inch dowel	4½ inches long
Leg caps	4	hollow rubber caps	see Notes on Materials
Glass	1	¹⁄₁₆-inch-thick clear glass	40¾ inches long x 8⅜ inches wide
Glass clips	10		see Notes on Materials
Hinges	2	spring-loaded concealed hinge	see Notes on Materials
Door handle	1	any style	

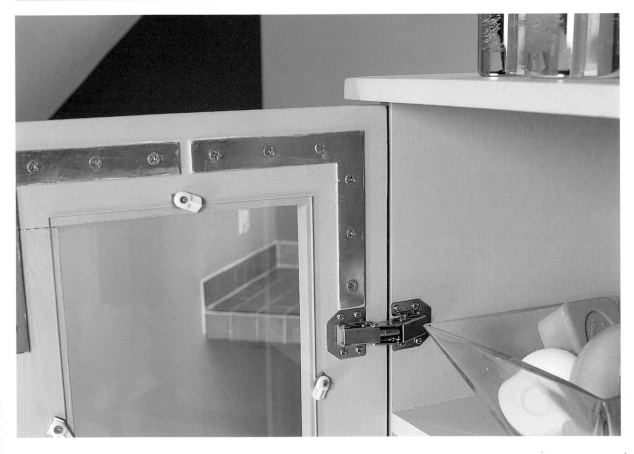

Tools

Measuring tape

Circular saw or miter saw

Cordless drill with drivers and bits

4 bar clamps, at least 48 inches long

Speed square or combination square

Random-orbit sander with pads from 60 to 220 grit

Eye and ear protection

Optional Tools

Table saw

Router

Fasteners

30 finish screws, 1⅜ inches long

9 finish nails, 1¼ inches long

30 brad nails, 1 inch long

4 square-drive deck screws, 1½ inches long

24 #8 wood screws, ½ inch long

Glue

Notes on Materials

The leg caps in the parts list are standard hollow rubber feet 1¹⁄₁₈ inches in diameter. You should be able to find them near the casters at your local building supply store. Since we don't have stops to which we can attach glazer's points, you'll need

glass clips that screw directly to the face of the door and cup the glass. Ask for these wherever you buy the glass. The concealed hinges chosen for this project don't need mortising. They install directly to the inside face of the door and the side of the cabinet. They are spring loaded so no door catch is needed. Choose hinges that are about 4 inches wide when open.

Instructions

Unless otherwise specified, joints are connected using three 1⅜-inch-long finish screws.

1 Cut the sides, base, and shelves of the box to size. Use a router, table saw, or circular saw outfitted with a rip guide to cut a rabbet ¼ inch deep x ½ inch wide along the back of both sides. Mark the sides for the shelves as shown in the plans. Clamp the two sides together and drill clearance holes for the shelves and base. Glue, clamp and screw the box together as configured in the drawing. The shelves should fit flush with the front of the sides and the rabbeted groove on the back of the sides (see photo A). Note: If rabbeting seems beyond your skill level, you can also attach the back directly to non-rabbeted sides. The only difference will be that the edge of the plywood back will be visible. If you go this route, use full-width 1x12 stock for the base and shelves.

RABBETED GROOVE. **Cut a rabbet along the back edge of each side. Set the shelves and base in place so that they are flush with the bottom of this groove.**

2 Cut the back. Lay the project face down on your worktable. Apply glue, set the back into the rabbeted groove, and nail it in place using 1-inch-long brad nails. Use eight evenly spaced nails on each side and three nails on each shelf (see photo B).

INSTALLING THE BACK. **Set the plywood back into the rabbeted grooves. The rabbet will conceal the back from sight, giving the cabinet a cleaner look.**

3 Cut the top and its front and side facing. Cut a 45-degree miter at each end of the front facing. Glue and clamp this piece to the front of the 1x12 top, as shown in the plans. Drill three $\frac{1}{16}$-inch pilot holes through the facing and into the 1x12, then attach the facing using 1$\frac{1}{4}$-inch finish nails. Make a butt cut at one end of each piece of side facing and a 45-degree miter cut at the other end, with the short point of the miter at 11$\frac{1}{4}$ inches. Glue and clamp these pieces to the ends of the 1x12 top, as shown in the drawing. Drill three $\frac{1}{16}$-inch pilot holes through the facing and into the top, then nail the facing in place with 1$\frac{1}{4}$-inch finish nails. Using a table saw, sliding miter saw, or circular saw, cut off the tip of the miters at each end of the $\frac{7}{8}$-inch-wide rip so that the two rips are flush at the corner, as seen in photo C and in the corner detail drawing on page 118.

FACING THE TOP. **The short ends of the miters meet at each corner of the 1x12 top. Cut the tips off the end of the miters on the front facing so that it is flush with the side facing.**

You may be wondering why we need to make this modified mitered joint. Well, we need to widen a 1x12 enough to allow the top to cover the door, so we have to add facing to the front of the top. Alone, that would give us both a visible joint and exposed end grain on the sides of the top. To avoid this, we add mitered facing to the sides. Note that the two pieces of facing are cut to different widths.

4 Install the top so that it's flush with the back of the cabinet and overhangs each side $\frac{1}{2}$ inch.

5 Cut the legs to length. Lay the project on its back and use a 1$\frac{1}{8}$-inch-diameter spade bit to drill four holes approximately $\frac{1}{2}$ inch deep into the base. The center of each hole should be 1$\frac{1}{4}$ inches from the side and 2$\frac{1}{2}$ inches from the end of each corner of the base. Push each leg into its hole and make a mark on the leg 3$\frac{1}{2}$ inches from the base. Keeping track of which leg goes in which hole, remove the legs and cut them at their respective 3$\frac{1}{2}$-inch marks. Apply glue and push each leg back into its hole. Using a speed square to make sure that the leg is square to the base, hold each leg in place

Bathroom Cabinet

and drill pilot holes for 1½-square-drive deck screws through the center of each hole and into the leg. Screw the legs into place, checking that each is oriented correctly with the speed square. Push the leg caps onto the bottom of each leg. (Note: if the cabinet needs to sit on a floor that isn't level, you can shim up a leg by placing a small piece of wood or cardboard into a cap to make one leg a bit longer.)

6 Cut the door rails and stiles to size. Apply glue to the joint edges and clamp the door together as configured in the plans. Set the corner braces in place as shown, then attach them with ½-inch wood screws (see photo D).

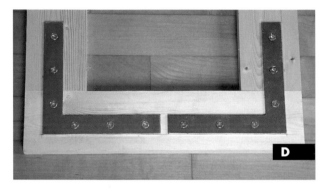

BUILDING THE DOOR. **Install corner braces to hold the door together and prevent warping.**

7 Fill any holes and imperfections with wood putty appropriate to your chosen finish and sand the project as described on page 28. Wipe off any sawdust with a tack cloth and finish the project as desired. The project pictured here was first covered with a coat of primer then finished with several coats of latex flat enamel paint. The project was sanded with 220-grit paper between each coat. The wooden legs were sprayed with a coat of primer and several coats of chrome paint.

8 Set the glass in place on the door as shown in the plans. Install three glass clips on each side and two at the top and bottom.

9 Install the hinges on the door as shown in the drawing. The hinges should be placed so that the side of the door will be flush with the outside face of the box. With the cabinet on its side, attach the hinges to the interior face of the side of the box. Position the hinges to allow a ⅛-inch gap between the door and the top and bottom of the cabinet.

10 Install your chosen door handle.

Notes on Installation

This cabinet has a thin profile and relatively heavy door—two variables that could cause the cabinet to tip over when the door is opened. For this reason, the cabinet should be permanently attached to a wall. This can be accomplished easily by screwing directly through the cabinet back into a structural wall member. See page 32 for general comments on wall mounting.

Desk

In this incarnation, our basic box sprouts legs. By adding three drawers, a simple exposed shelf unit, and a handsome top, we've created a stylish desk with a lot of storage capacity. To build it, you won't need any new skills, but we do step up the precision meter one more notch. As you can see, I designed these drawers so that they close flush with the sides of the desk and with no gap between them. But this detail is only a small challenge that comes at the very end of an otherwise straightforward project.

Desk Plans

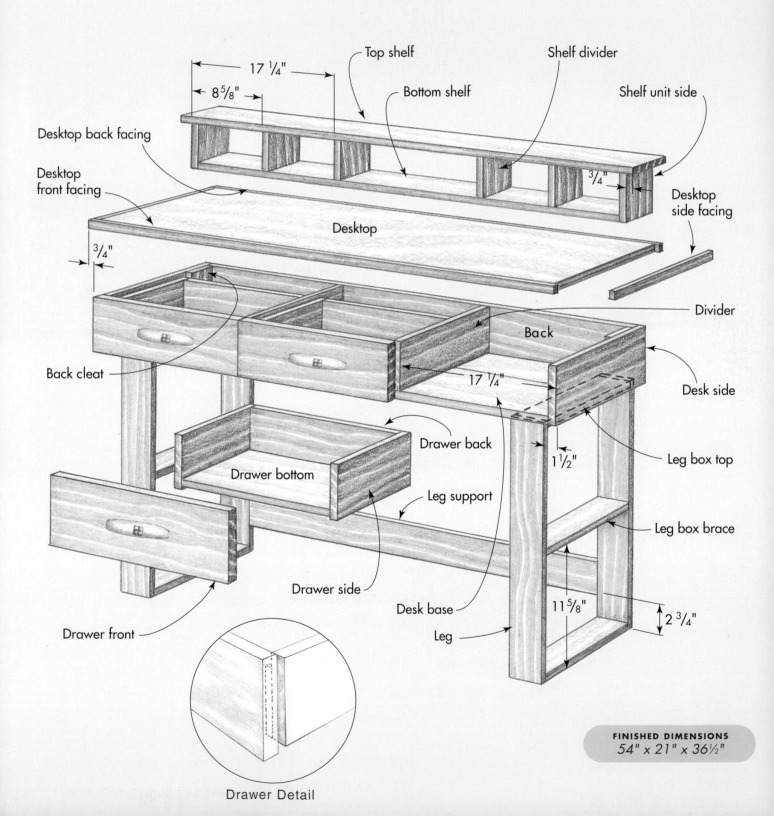

17 1/4"

8 5/8"

Top shelf

Bottom shelf

Shelf divider

Shelf unit side

Desktop back facing

Desktop front facing

3/4"

Desktop

3/4"

Desktop side facing

Divider

Back

Back cleat

17 1/4"

Desk side

Leg box top

1 1/2"

Drawer back

Drawer bottom

Leg support

Leg box brace

Drawer side

Desk base

11 5/8"

2 3/4"

Drawer front

Leg

FINISHED DIMENSIONS
54" x 21" x 36½"

Drawer Detail

Parts List

Part	Qty.	Material	Dimensions
Legs	4	1x4 pine	24 inches long
Leg box brace	2	1x4 pine	16 inches long
Leg box top	2	1x4 pine	16 inches long
Desk sides	2	1x6 pine	18 ½ inches long
Desk base	2	1x10 pine	51 inches long
Desktop	1	¾-inch high-grade plywood, capped with 1x stock	20 ¼ inches x 53 ¼ inches
Desktop front facing	1	any 1x stock	ripped to ⅜ inch wide x 54 inches long
Desktop back facing	1	any 1x stock	ripped to ⅜ inch wide x 54 inches long
Desktop side facing	2	any 1x stock	ripped to ⅜ inch wide x 20 ¼ inch long
Desk dividers	2	1x6 pine	ripped to 4 ¾ inches wide x 17 ¾ inches long
Leg support	1	1x4 pine	42 ½ inches long
Bottom shelf	1	1x6 pine	51 inches long
Shelf unit sides	2	1x6 pine	5 ½ inches long
Shelf dividers	4	1x6 pine	4 ¾ inches long
Top shelf	1	1x8 pine	ripped to 6 ½ inches wide x 54 inches long
Drawer sides	6	1x6 pine	ripped to 4 ½ inches wide x 15 inches long
Drawer back	3	1x6 pine	ripped to 4 ⅜ inches wide x 14 ⅞ inches long
Drawer bottom	3	¾ CDX plywood	14 ⅞ x 14 ¼ inches
Drawer front	3	1x6 pine	17 ⅝ inches long
Back cleats	2	1x6 pine	ripped to 4 ¾ inches wide x 2 ½ inches long
Desk back	1	1x6 pine	ripped to 4 ¾ inches wide x 51 inches long
Drawer pulls	3	any style	

Tools

- Measuring tape
- Circular saw or miter saw
- Cordless drill with drivers and bits
- Speed square or combination square
- 4 bar clamps, at least 24 inches long
- Random-orbit sander with pads from 60 to 220 grit
- Eye and ear protection

Optional Tools

- Table saw
- 2 bar clamps, at least 6 feet long

Fasteners

- 150 finish screws, 1⅝ inches long
- 30 finish nails, 1 inch long
- 16 wood screws, 1¼ inches long
- 10 finish nails, 1¼ inches long
- Glue

Notes on Materials

By high-grade plywood, I mean any plywood that has a smooth surface without blemishes. These grades of plywood, sometimes called *finish plywood*, are designed to be used in furniture and cabinetry in situations where their faces will be seen. For this project, I chose a birch finish plywood for its interesting grain pattern.

Instructions

As I mentioned in the introduction to this project, the drawer fronts are the challenge in this project. In fact, it's really a simple joinery job, but all of those $7/16$- and $13/16$-inch dimensions can make it seem confusing. Just make sure you understand the layout before you start connecting the drawer fronts. Build the drawers one at a time, check the Parts List dimensions against your real project, and make small adjustments as necessary. Unless otherwise specified, all joints are connected with $1\frac{5}{8}$-inch finish screws.

1 Cut all pieces to make up the leg boxes: legs, bases, braces, and tops. Drill two clearance holes for each joint, then glue, clamp and screw the leg boxes together, as configured in the plans.

2 Cut desk base pieces, sides, and dividers to size. Edge-glue the base pieces together to make one wide board. (For more on this technique, see the storage chest project on page 112.) Drill four clearance holes for each side joint and six clearance holes through the base for each divider. Glue, clamp, and screw together the base, sides, and dividers.

3 Cut the desktop and all desktop facing. Glue and clamp both pieces of side facing to the shorter sides of the plywood and attach them using 1-inch-long finish nails spaced every 6 inches apart. Glue and clamp the front and back facing to the longer sides of the plywood, making sure they're flush with the outside edges of the side fac-

ing. Secure the front and back facing with 1-inch-long finish nails spaced every 6 inches apart.

4 Attach the desktop to the sides and dividers. Drill four clearance holes for each joint then glue and screw the top in place. As shown in the illustrations, the top should overhang the sides and back ¾ inch. The front side of the top should overhang the desk box 1½ inches.

5 Clean off your worktable and cover it with soft cloth to protect the desktop, then lay the desktop facedown on the table. Apply glue and attach the leg boxes. Each leg box should be inset 1½ inch from the sides and inset ½ inch from the front and back of the desk base. Drill pairs of pilot holes for 1¼-inch wood screws through the leg box into the base. Use eight screws to secure each leg box.

6 Cut the leg support to length. With the desk still laying on its face, glue and clamp the leg support in place. After predrilling for a finish screw, sink a toenailed screw through the bottom edge of the leg support into each back leg. Set the desk onto its legs and toenail screws through the top edge of the leg support in the same fashion (see photo A).

ATTACHING THE LEG SUPPORT. **Toenail the leg support in place with 1⅝-inch finish screws. This support will brace the two leg boxes together, keeping them square and preventing them from spreading.**

7 Cut the bottom shelf, shelf sides, and dividers to size. Drill two clearance holes for each joint, then glue, clamp, and screw the sides and dividers to the bottom shelf. Apply glue and attach the bottom shelf to the desktop. The shelf should be flush with the back of the desktop and set in at each end by ¾ inch. After predrilling pilot holes, toenail two finish screws through the shelf so that they pass through the top and into the desk sides and dividers. If there are places where the bottom shelf isn't tight against the desktop, nail the shelf down in these spots using 1¼-inch finish nails.

8 Cut the top shelf, then drill two clearance holes for each joint. Glue and screw the top shelf in place. The back side of the shelf should be flush with the backs of the sides and dividers. The ends of the top shelf should overhang the shelf unit sides by ¾ of an inch.

9 Cut the drawer sides, bottoms, and backs to size. For each side, drill four clearance holes to attach the bottom and two to attach the back. Glue, clamp, and screw each drawer together. The drawer backs should be flush with the top of the sides. The bottoms are attached flush with the bottom of the backs, setting them ⅛ inch higher than the drawer sides. This will cause less friction and allow the drawers to open and close more freely.

DRAWER FRONT DETAILS. **If you choose to stain or clear-coat your desk, consider cutting the drawer fronts out of a single piece of lumber with an interesting grain, then orient them to create the feel of one large seamless face. Notice the ⅟₁₆-inch gap between the top of the drawer front and the bottom of the desktop.**

10 Cut the drawer fronts to size (see photo B). Unlike in other projects, these drawer fronts are designed to close with a little gap exposed between the drawer fronts and the dividers. For this reason, the sides of each drawer front are positioned a bit differently in relation to the drawer. To help you position the drawer fronts, see the plans.

On the drawer fronts, drill two clearance holes on both sides and another two at the bottom. Attach the fronts to the drawer boxes. Glue, clamp, and screw the drawer fronts in place. When all is said and done, each installed drawer front will be centered on a divider, but the outside edges of the left

and right drawer fronts will be flush with the sides of the desk. There should be a 1/16-inch gap between the tops of the faces and underside of the desktop. The bottoms of the drawer fronts will extend past the desk base by 1/16 inch (see photo C).

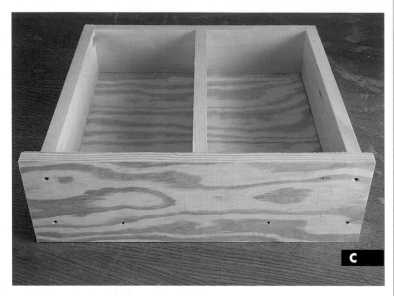

C

ATTACHING THE DRAWER FRONTS. **Each drawer front has a different relationship to the drawer. The left drawer, seen here, has the front oriented so that it overhangs the left drawer side by 13/16 inch, but there is only a 7/16-inch overhang on the right where it abuts the center drawer front. These drawers are large, so you may want to consider installing center dividers to allow for more organization, as shown here.**

11 Cut the desk back and the back cleats. Apply glue and attach the cleats to the desk sides, 3/4 inch in from the back corner of the desk, using 1 1/4-inch finish nails placed (see photo D). Apply glue and set the desk back in place against the cleats. Attach the back to the cleats and dividers with two finish screws per joint. Drill pilot holes for each screw.

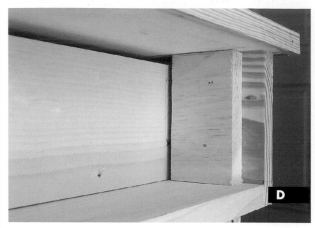

D

INSTALLING THE BACK. **Attach the back cleats 3/4 inch in from the back corners of the desk, then set the desk back in place and attach it to the cleats and dividers.**

12 Fill any holes and imperfections with wood putty appropriate to your chosen finish and sand the project as described on page 28. Wipe off all sawdust with a tack cloth and finish the project as desired. The project pictured was first covered with an oil-based wood conditioner then two coats of a pecan-tinted oil-based stain, which was applied with a rag. Finally, a coat of oil-based, high-gloss clear polyurethane was used to seal the project.

13 Install the drawer pulls of your choice.

Kitchen Cart

Even in this book's arguably most advanced project, the basic box is still clearly visible. I've added strong legs, casters, four drawers, homemade industrial handles, and a durable top made of hardwood flooring. To build it, you won't need any completely new skills. Things such as facing plywood edges, building low-friction drawers, and toenail fastening have been introduced elsewhere. You'll use only basic butt joints and most are fastened with your old friend, the finish screw. The end result is a kitchen cart built like a tank. It has large open storage for pots and pans, big sturdy drawers that can hold large cans or other heavy items, and smaller drawers for silverware, utensils, knives, and the like.

Kitchen Cart Plans

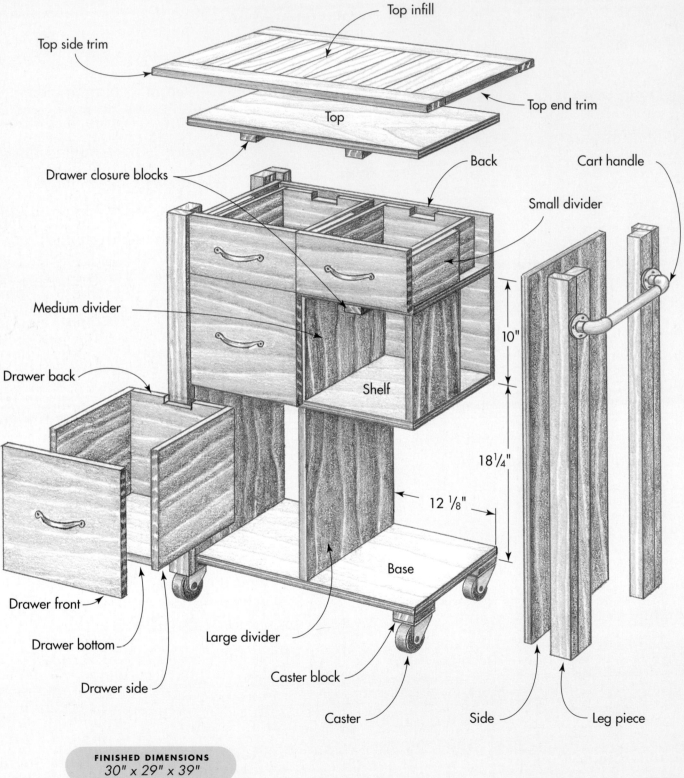

Top infill

Top side trim

Top end trim

Top

Drawer closure blocks

Back

Cart handle

Small divider

Medium divider

10"

Drawer back

Shelf

Drawer front

18¼"

Large divider

12 ⅛"

Base

Drawer bottom

Caster block

Drawer side

Caster

Side

Leg piece

FINISHED DIMENSIONS
30" x 29" x 39"

Parts List

Part	Qty.	Material	Dimensions
Sides	2	¾-inch high-finish plywood	34½ x 15½ inches
Base	1	¾-inch finish plywood, capped with 1x stock	23½ x 15½ inches
Shelves	2	¾-inch plywood	23½ x 14¾ inches
Large divider	1	¾-inch finish plywood, capped with 1x stock	18 x 15½ inches
Medium divider	3	1x10 pine	9¼ inches long
Small divider	3	1x10 pine	5 inches long
Top	1	¾-inch CDX plywood, capped with 1x stock	25 x 15½ inches
Back	1	¾-inch finish plywood	23½ x 15¾ inches
Leg pieces	8	2x4 pine	ripped to 2¼ inches wide x 36 inches long
Caster blocks	4	¾ plywood	2¼ inches long x ¾ inches wide
Casters	4	plastic wheeled casters, at least one that can lock	2½ inches in diameter
Top side trim	2	1x4 pine	30 inches long
Top end trim	2	1x4 pine	13 inches long
Top infill	11	¾-inch tongue-and-groove hardwood flooring	2¼ inches wide x 13 inches long
Large drawer sides	4	1x10 pine	ripped to 9 inches wide x 14 inches long
Large drawer back	2	1x10 pine	ripped to 8⅞ inches wide x 9 inches long
Large drawer front	2	1x12 pine	ripped to 10 inches wide x 11⅜ long
Small drawer sides	4	1x6 pine	ripped to 4¾ inches wide x 14 inches long
Small drawer back	2	1x6 pine	ripped to 4⅝ inches wide x 9 inches long
Small drawer front	2	1x8 pine	ripped to 5¾ inches wide x 11⅜ inches long
Drawer bottoms	4	¾-inch CDX plywood	9 x 13¼ inches
Drawer closure blocks	4	¾-inch CDX plywood	1 inch wide x 1¾ inches long
Drawer pulls	4	any style	
Cart handles	2	any style	

Tools

Measuring tape

Circular saw or miter saw

Cordless drill with drivers and bits

Speed square or combination square

4 bar clamps, at least 48 inches long

Hand saw

1½-inch chisel

Random-orbit sander with pads from 60 to 220 grit

Eye and ear protection

Optional Tools

Table saw

Jigsaw

Fasteners

200 finish screws, 1⅝ inches long

60 finish screws, 2¼ inches long

35 finish nails, 1 inch long

60 finish nails, 1¼ inches long

20 square-drive deck screws, 1¼ inches long

16 wood screws, 1 inch long

Glue

Notes on Materials

As the name implies, tongue-and-groove flooring has a groove milled into one side and a protruding tongue on the other. The grooves of one piece fit over the tongues of another, creating tight joints. I chose maple hardwood flooring for this project, but most species will work fine. In my experience, the most common flooring at the big building supply stores is oak. Just make sure you buy solid wood flooring, not laminates. Hardwood flooring usually comes in small bundles with boards of varying lengths. Unless you leave the flooring lumber completely natural without any kind of finish, I don't suggest using it as a cutting board. Some natural oils go rancid, and some can even be toxic.

See Notes on Materials on page 126 of the desk project for a description of finish plywood.

Instructions

All Parts Lists dimensions are based on plywood with an actual thickness of ¾ inch. If your plywood is thinner, you'll need to adjust the project dimensions accordingly. Unless otherwise specified, all joints are connected with four 1⅝-inch finish screws.

1 A number of the parts in this project are plywood-faced with 1x stock to cover their raw edges. It's easiest to cut all of these parts now. First, rip 15 linear feet of ¼-inch-wide 1x stock. As you cut the plywood parts to size, cut the facing to length, then glue, clamp, and attach it using 1-inch-long finish nails spaced every 6 inches.

To make the base, cut a 23½ x 15-inch piece of finish plywood and face the 23½-inch-long sides with edging. To make the shelves, cut 23½ x 14½-inch pieces of finish plywood and face one long side. To make the large divider, cut an 18 x 15-inch piece of finish plywood and face the 18-inch-long sides. To make the top, cut a 24½ x 15-inch piece of finish plywood and face all four sides.

2 Cut the sides, medium dividers, and small dividers to size. Using the dimensions provided in the plans, drill four clearance holes through the sides for the base and shelves. Glue, clamp, and fasten the base, shelves, and dividers in place. The shelves are installed with the faced sides flush with the front of the box. This will create a ¾-inch-deep pocket at the rear side of the cart to accommodate the back.

Attach the base first, then the lower shelf. Attach the large divider next by driving four finish screws directly through the base and first shelf. Apply glue and clamp a medium divider flush with the front of each side piece. Place these dividers so that the end grain faces the shelves, and attach each of them with two pairs of 1¼-inch finish nails.

Next, install the second shelf. Set the middle medium divider flush with front of the box then drive two 1⅜-inch-long finish screws directly through the second shelf into the divider. Also, toenail two 1⅜-inch-long screws through the bottom of the first shelf and into the divider. Apply glue and clamp a small divider flush with the front of each side piece as shown in the drawing. Attach each of these dividers with two pairs of 1¼-inch finish nails.

Install the top so that it caps the sides. Drill four pilot holes for each side and attach the ends of the top to the sides of the cart. Next, drive two 1⅜-inch-long finish screws directly through the top, and sink them into the medium divider. Attach the bottom of the middle small divider with two toenailed screws, as you did for the middle medium divider (see photo A).

3 Cut the back to size. Apply glue and set it in place on top of the large divider and against the back of the shelves, as shown in the plans. Drill five pilot holes for 1⅜-inch-long finish screws through the back and into each shelf, then another five through the top and into the back. Screw the back into place.

4 To make the legs, rip 24 linear feet of 2x4 twice: once to remove the rounded edge, then again to bring it down to 2¼ inches wide. All eight leg pieces are cut from this stock, and it's best to cut all of the stock before you assemble the legs. To make the legs, drill six evenly spaced pilot holes for 2¼-inch-long finish screws, ¾ inch in from one edge of each leg. Glue, clamp, and screw the predrilled legs to the thickness of the other legs to create four L-shaped leg assemblies (see photo B).

INSTALLING THE DIVIDERS. **The second shelf is sandwiched between the medium and small dividers at the side of the box. The endgrain of the sides will be covered by the leg assemblies, and these dividers will form the boxes that house the drawers.**

ATTACHING THE LEGS. **Attach the leg assemblies so that they wrap the front and back of the box, covering the end grain on the side pieces. They should be flush with the top of the box and overhang the bottom by ¾ inch.**

5 Glue and clamp the leg assemblies in place as shown in the plans. The tops of the legs should be flush with the top of the box but overhang the bottom by ¾ inch (see photo B on page 133). The assemblies should wrap around the front and back of the box sides, covering the endgrain. Drill five pilot holes through the front of the leg assemblies into the endgrain of the sides of the box, then attach them using 2¼-inch finish screws. After drilling six pilot holes per leg, screw the leg assemblies to the sides of the box. Use 2¼-inch finish screws wherever a screw will be entering a divider. Otherwise, use 1⅝-inch screws and be sure to countersink them.

6 Flip the cart over so that the top is face-down on the floor. Apply glue and set the caster blocks in place. Drill pilot holes for 1¼-inch deck screws through each caster block, then screw them in place.

7 Set the cart on its wheels and engage the lock on the locking caster. Cut the top side and end trim pieces. Glue, clamp, and install both side trim pieces and one end trim piece as shown in the plans. Secure them in place with 1¼-inch finish nails. The trim should overhang the leg assemblies by ¾ inch on all sides.

8 Cut the hardwood flooring infill. Rip 1 inch off the grooved side of a piece of flooring. Apply glue, and set this piece flush against the end trim. Drill ⅛-inch toenailed pilot holes through the hardwood flooring, starting at the top of the tongue. Drill a hole 1 inch in from each end of the piece and one in the middle of the board. Drive a 1¼-inch finish nail through the hole until its head sticks up about ¹⁄₁₆ inch, then use a nail set to bury it below the surface of the flooring (see photo C). Apply glue and set the next piece in place with its tongue locking into the groove of the previously installed piece. Continue installing the flooring in this manner (see

photo D). Before installing the final piece, draw a line on the top of the box 3½ inches in from the ends of the side trim pieces. The inside edge of the end trim will be installed on this line. Measure from this line to the outside edge of the last piece of flooring installed. Rip the final flooring piece to this width. Install the final piece of flooring. Apply glue and install the last piece of trim as you did earlier.

9 Cut the drawer sides, bottoms, and backs to size. Glue and clamp the drawers together as illustrated in the drawing. Attach the joints with 1⅝-inch finish screws. The drawer backs should be attached flush with the top of the sides. The bottoms are attached flush with the bottom of the backs.

INSTALLING THE HARDWOOD FLOORING INFILL. **Apply glue and set the groove of each piece of flooring over the tongue of the previous piece (C). Toenail through the hardwood floor, starting just above the tongue, and set the nail just below the surface (D).**

When joined, the bottom should be ⅛ inch higher than the drawer sides. This will allow the long drawers to open and close easily, because only the sides will rub against the base. Using a jigsaw or a hand saw and chisel, cut a 1-inch-wide x 1½-inch-long notch in the center of the edge of each drawer back (see photo E). These notches will accommodate the drawer closure blocks.

PREP THE DRAWERS FOR CLOSURE BLOCKS. **Cut a 1-inch-wide x 1½-inch-long notch in the center of each drawer back. These notches will accommodate the drawer closure block.**

10 Cut the drawer fronts to size. Once installed there should be a ¼-inch reveal between every drawer front and the surface next to it. To accomplish this, attach the lower drawer fronts so that they overhang the bottom by ½ inch and the top by ⅜ inch. Attach the small drawer faces so that they overhang the bottom by ¼ inch and the top by ¼ inch. The sides of all drawer fronts should overhang each drawer side by ⁵⁄₁₆ inch. Glue and clamp the faces into place. Drill two pilot holes for the bottom and each side, then attach the fronts with 1⅝-inch finish screws.

11 Cut the drawer closure blocks to size. Drill a single clearance hole for a 1¼-inch deck screw ¼ inch in from one end of each block. Screw the blocks in place centered in each drawer opening, as shown in the plans. Turn them so that their 1-inch side faces out. Push the drawers into each opening

until the notch in the back of the drawer passes the closure block, then turn the closure block 90 degrees. These closure blocks will make it impossible to pull the drawer all the way out. To remove the drawer, simply flip them back in the other direction.

12 Fill any holes and imperfections with wood putty appropriate to your finish, then sand the project as described on page 28. You may have to go at the hardwood top with 60-grit paper to get all the bumps out. Still, the small area of the top shouldn't take more than a few minutes to sand. Wipe off all sawdust with a tack cloth and finish the project as desired. The project pictured here was covered with an oil-based satin polyurethane. It was then sanded with 220-grit paper and covered with a second coat of polyurethane. Finally, it was sanded with 400-grit wet/dry sandpaper.

13 Install the drawer pulls and cart handles of your choice. The handles need to be face-mounted and very sturdy because this is a heavy piece of furniture. I made our handles out of ½-inch galvanized pipe. At a local builder's supply, I had two pieces cut to 13¼ inches long and threaded at both ends. I then attached 90-degree elbows, 1-inch-long nipples, and floor flanges to each end of the pipes. I placed each handle centered on the leg assemblies and about 2 inches below the bottom of the top trim. The handles are attached through the holes in the flanges using 1-inch-long wood screws.

Wardrobe

At its core, this project is just a basic box with a couple of shelves and a few added accessories. What lends it a bit of refinement is the careful selection of materials and simple, yet effective trim choices. The challenge for the fledgling furniture maker traveling through this book is going to be the scale. This is a full-size piece of furniture. The individual pieces are heavy and often unruly. To help you out, I've kept the design clean, using only butt cuts and basic joinery. The finished wardrobe is divided into two sides. Each side has a large compartment for shoes, a hanging area to accommodate long coats, and a top compartment for storing hats, gloves, or any smaller items.

Wardrobe Plans

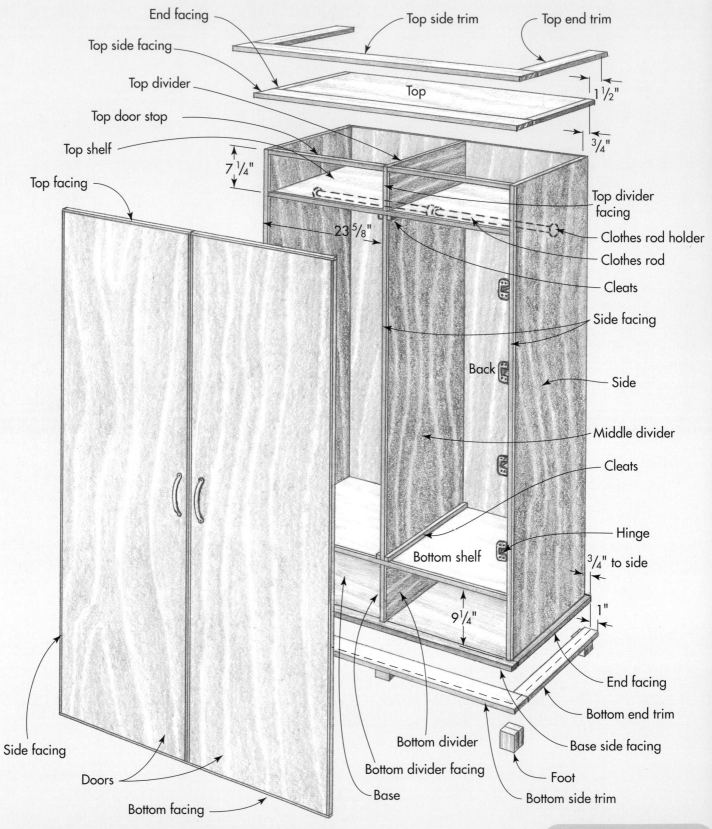

End facing

Top side facing

Top divider

Top door stop

Top shelf

Top facing

Top side trim

Top end trim

1 1/2"

Top

3/4"

7 1/4"

23 5/8"

Top divider facing

Clothes rod holder

Clothes rod

Cleats

Side facing

Back

Side

Middle divider

Cleats

Hinge

Bottom shelf

3/4" to side

1"

9 1/4"

Side facing

Doors

Bottom facing

Bottom divider

Bottom divider facing

Base

End facing

Bottom end trim

Base side facing

Foot

Bottom side trim

FINISHED DIMENSIONS
52 1/2" x 27" x 77 1/4"

Parts List

Part	Qty.	Material	Dimensions
Top	1	¾-inch high-grade plywood	23¼ inches x 48 inches
Base	1	¾-inch high-grade plywood	23¼ inches x 48 inches
Sides	2	¾-inch high-grade plywood	23½ inches x 72 inches
Back	1	¼-inch lauan plywood	47⁷⁄₁₆ inches x 72 inches
End facings	4	1x stock	ripped to ¾ inches wide x 23½ inches long
Base side facing	1	1x stock	ripped to 1¼ inches wide x 49½ inches long
Top side facing	1	1x stock	ripped to 2 inches wide x 49½ inches long
Top side trim	1	1x6 pine	52½ inches long
Top end trim	2	1x4 pine	21½ inches long
Bottom side trim	1	1x4 pine	51½ inches long
Bottom end trim	2	1x4 pine	22¼ inches long
Feet	6	2x4 pine	3 inches long x 3 inches wide x 3 inches thick
Top shelf	1	¾-inch high-grade plywood	23¼ inches wide x 46½ inches long
Bottom shelf	1	¾-inch high-grade plywood	23¼ inches wide x 46½ inches long
Top divider	1	1x8 pine	23¼ inches long
Bottom divider	1	1x10 pine	23¼ inches long
Middle divider	1	¾-inch high-grade plywood	23¼ inches wide x 54 inches long
Cleats	4	1x stock	ripped to ¾ inches wide x 23¼ inches long
Side facing	2	1x stock	ripped to ¼ inches wide x 72 inches long
Shelf facing	2	1x stock	ripped to ¼ inches wide x 46½ inches long
Top divider facing	1	1x stock	ripped to ¼ inches wide x 7¼ inches long
Middle divider facing	1	1x stock	ripped to ¼ inches wide x 54 inches long
Bottom divider facing	1	1x stock	ripped to ¼ inches wide x 9¼ inches long
Clothes rod holders	4		see Notes on Materials
Clothes rods	2	wood dowel	4 feet long; see Notes on Materials
Top door stops	2	1x stock	ripped to 1¼ inches wide x 22⅞ inches long
Doors	2	¾-inch high-grade plywood	69¾ x 23⅜ inches
Door side facing	4	1x stock	ripped to ¼ inch wide x 69¾ inches long
Door bottom facing	2	1x stock	ripped to ¼ inch wide x 23⅞ inches long
Door top facing	2	1x stock	ripped to ½ inch wide x 23⅞ inches long
Hinges	8	spring-loaded concealed hinge	See Notes on Materials
Door handles	2	any style	
Door catches	2	sturdy magnetic variety	

Tools

Measuring tape

Circular saw or miter saw

Cordless drill with drivers and bits

Speed square or combination square

Framing square

4 bar clamps, at least 48 inches long

Random-orbit sander with pads from 60 to 220 grit

Eye and ear protection

Optional Tools

Table saw

Router

Fasteners

60 finish screws, $1\frac{5}{8}$ inches long

125 finish nails, 1 inch long

30 finish nails, $1\frac{1}{2}$ inches long

60 finish nails, $1\frac{1}{4}$ inches long

1 carriage bolt with nut and washer, $\frac{3}{16}$ inch in diameter and 1 inch long

Glue

Notes on Materials

You'll need two sets of clothes rod holders. I recommend looking for wooden holders that that have a single hole through the center for a single screw. Buy 4 feet of wooden dowel of the appropriate diameter to fit the holders.

The concealed hinges chosen for this project don't need mortising. They install directly to the inside face of the door and the side of the cabinet. Even though they are spring-loaded, I recommend using them in combination with magnetic door catches.

When choosing hinges, be sure that the hinges you choose will allow the doors to overlay the sides completely.

Instructions

If you aren't accustomed to wrestling with heavy things, be careful as you navigate this project. Remember the tried and true rule: "Use your legs, not your back." Other than that, the big challenge here is hanging the large doors symmetrically—making sure they operate smoothly and have even reveals on all sides. As long as you take care installing the hinges, everything will turn out fine. Unless otherwise instructed, use three $1\frac{5}{8}$-inch-long finish screws to fasten each joint.

1 Cut the sides, top, and base to size. Use a router, table saw, or circular saw to cut a $\frac{1}{4}$-inch-deep x $\frac{1}{2}$-inch-wide rabbet along the back of both sides. (See page 121 for a photo of this same cut on the bathroom cabinet.) Drill clearance holes $\frac{3}{8}$ inch in from both ends of the top and base. Referring to the plans, apply glue and assemble the box with its front face on the floor. The top and base should cover the end grain on the sides. The top and base should be flush with the bottom of the rabbets in the back.

2 Cut the back to size. Apply glue to the rabbets in the sides and set the back in place. Your box may be out of square at this point so you may need to push on one corner or another to fit the back into place. Once attached, the back will bring the box into square. Attach the back using 1-inch finish nails spaced every 6 inches.

3 Turn the wardrobe over onto its back. Cut the end, top side, and base side facing to width and length. Referring to the drawing, apply glue and attach all of the facing.

4 Cut all of the trim pieces to size. Glue, clamp, and nail the pieces in place as shown in the plans. Use pairs of $1\frac{1}{4}$-inch finish nails spaced about

12 inches apart. The top trim should be placed so that it overhangs the top by 1½ inch. The base trim should overhang the base above it by 1 inch.

5 To make the feet, rip 38 inches of 2 x 4 to 3 inches wide, then cut the board into twelve 3-inch-long pieces. Join the pieces together in pairs by gluing and nailing them together using 1¼-inch finish nails. Referring to the plans, apply glue and attach the feet by screwing directly through the base with 1⅝-inch finish screws. To prevent the feet from wiggling loose, use two screws per foot. The front corner feet are set into the corner created by the base trim. The back corner feet are aligned flush with the base trim and the back of the wardrobe. The two middle feet are centered across the width of the wardrobe.

6 Cut the shelves to length. The Parts List dimensions are based on a plywood top and base with an actual thickness of ¾ inches. Your plywood may be slightly thinner. If so, adjust your shelf length to compensate. After drilling clearance holes, glue, clamp, and screw the shelves into place as shown in the drawing.

7 Cut the top and bottom dividers. Glue, clamp, and screw them in place in the exact middle of the box.

8 Cut the side, shelf, and top and bottom divider facing to size. To cover the raw edges of the plywood, install the facing to each piece using 1-inch finish nails spaced about every 12 inches (see photo A).

9 Cut the middle divider as well as its facing and cleats. Apply glue and install the facing to the front edge of the divider using 1-inch finish nails spaced about every 12 inches. Drill three ¹⁄₁₆-inch pilot holes through each cleat. Apply glue and nail the two cleats used to support the left side of the middle divider as shown in the drawing. Apply glue to the side of the cleats and set the middle divider in place. Apply glue to the bottom and sides of the

MULTIPLE OVERHANGS. The simple technique of facing raw edges and creating dramatic overhangs gives you a lot of style with a minimum of effort.

remaining two cleats and nail them into the shelf flush against the right side of the middle divider. (see photo B).

10 Referring to the plans, glue and install the clothes rod holders in each of the two compartments. The holders should be centered in the middle of the wardrobe so that the top of the clothes rod will rest 1½ inches from the bottom of the top shelf. Drill pilot holes and attach the outside holders with appropriate screws. Since the two middle holders are placed directly across from each other on either side of the middle divider, apply glue and fasten them to the divider with a single carriage bolt ³⁄₁₆ inch in diameter and 1 inch long. If necessary, drill a clearance hole through the divider and the holders.

ATTACHING THE MIDDLE DIVIDER. Attach the middle divider by sandwiching it between two cleats.

11 Cut the top door stops to size. Apply glue and install them onto the underside of the top, flush with the face of the side and middle divider facings. Use three 1¼-inch finish nails for each stop. When closed, the doors will rest against the sides, middle divider, and these door stops.

12 Cut the door panels and all door facing to size. Use the same method used to cut the side panels. Glue, clamp, and nail the facing to the panels using 1-inch finish nails, just as you did on the sides, shelves, and dividers.

13 To attach the doors, first set them face down on your worktable. Attach the hinges so that the side of each door will be flush with the outside face of the wardrobe once installed. Place the top and bottom hinges about 6 inches from the top and bottom of the doors. Evenly space the other two hinges between the first two, then stand the wardrobe on its feet. Set a door next to the wardrobe as if it was attached and open. Prop the door up on a stack of wood scraps and shims until there is a ⅛-inch gap between the top of the door and the top side facing. Attach the hinges to the interior face of each side of the wardrobe. There

should be two longer holes in each hinge, which will allow for adjustment after the screws are in place. Attach screws into these two holes in each hinge first. If the door hangs correctly, go back and screw through the other holes. If it needs slight adjustment, loosen the screws in the long holes, move the door, and retighten the screws. Repeat this process with the other door (see photo C).

14 Nail the back of the wardrobe to the shelves and dividers with 1-inch finish nails spaced every 6 inches.

15 Install the door handles of your choice. I recommend also installing sturdy magnetic door catches. Place one directly under the top shelf on both sides of the middle divider.

16 Fill any holes and imperfections with wood putty appropriate to your chosen finish. Sand all plywood surfaces with 150- or 220-grit paper. You may need to start with a coarse grain on the facings and trim before ending with 150 or 220 grit. Wipe off all sawdust with a tack cloth and finish the project as desired. The project pictured here was first covered with an oil-based wood conditioner then a single coat of cherry-tinted, oil-based stain was applied with a rag. A coat of clear oil-based satin polyurethane was used to seal the project.

HANGING THE DOORS. **Hang the doors so that they are flush with the outer edges of the wardrobe. This will create a ⅛-inch gap between the two doors and allow them to open and close freely. The line created by this gap is also a major design element, so hang the doors carefully.**

ABOUT THE AUTHORS

Clarke Snell has spent most of his life learning how to "do it yourself." He designed and constructed his first functional piece of wood furniture at the age of eight. It was a birdhouse built in the woodshop of the Eagle's Nest Summer Camp after a half-hearted attempt at leather wallet-making. Since then he has built many things (from furniture to houses), using many materials (from clay to straw to wood to metal to you name it). The driving force through it all has been his desire to decide exactly what is needed and make it, rather than look-

ing for something already made to fulfill a generic need; that, he believes, is what "doing it yourself" is all about. He is also the author of two books on house construction, *The Good House Book: A Common Sense Guide to Alternative Homebuilding* (Lark, 2004) and *Building Green: A Complete How-to Guide to Alternative Building Methods* (Lark Books, 2006).

Lisa Mandle has been painting, drawing, sewing, singing, and dancing her entire life. In her day job she's a clothing designer. She's created her own designs and patterns since receiving a BA in Fine Art from The Maryland Institute College of Art in 1983. She recently published a new pattern with Folkwear patterns and has taught pattern making to many. Her greatest accomplishment to date has been her nearly twenty-year partnership with husband/creative partner Clarke Snell. Together, they have created everything from avant-garde theater to an intentional community to the designing, construction, and finishing of their owner-built home and gardens. To the projects of this book, she lent her talent for design and sketching as well as her particular flair for color in the selected finishes.

METRIC CONVERSION CHART

Inches	Centimeters	Inches	Centimeters
1/8	3 mm	12	30
1/4	6 mm	13	32.5
3/8	9 mm	14	35
1/2	1.3	15	37.5
5/8	1.6	16	40
3/4	1.9	17	42.5
7/8	2.2	18	45
1	2.5	19	47.5
1 1/4	3.1	20	50
1 1/2	3.8	21	52.5
1 3/4	4.4	22	55
2	5	23	57.5
2 1/2	6.25	24	60
3	7.5	25	62.5
3 1/2	8.8	26	65
4	10	27	67.5
4 1/2	11.3	28	70
5	12.5	29	72.5
5 1/2	13.8	30	75
6	15	31	77.5
7	17.5	32	80
8	20	33	82.5
9	22.5	34	85
10	25	35	87.5
11	27.5	36	90

ACKNOWLEDGMENTS

Tim Callahan is a master woodworker who has built everything from guitars to fine furniture to million-dollar yachts to custom homes. He was an invaluable help in the design and construction planning of these projects. He also has the best laugh you'll ever hear.

Suzanne Tourtillott was our patient project manager with the calming phone voice. In addition to being organization central, she was a huge help in honing the designs and choosing the project finishes.

Our editor **Matthew Teague** had the difficult job of coming on board long after this book was underway. His diligence and hard work is much appreciated.

We were lucky enough to merit our old friend **Dana Irwin** as art director. To experience her skill and creativity, refer to any page in this book.

Stewart O'Shields did all of the photography of the finished projects. Not only does he do beautiful work, but he's fun to work with.

And thanks once again to **Carol Taylor**, **Deborah Morgenthal**, and the entire well-oiled machine that is Lark Books.

INDEX